The Torch Carrier (A Poetic Saga of Love)

By

Antonio Richardson

ISBN: 1-4107-9696-5 (e-book)
ISBN: 1-4107-9697-3 (Paperback)
ISBN: 1-4107-9698-1 (Dust Jacket)

Library of Congress Control Number: 2003098480

This book is printed on acid free paper.

Printed in the United States of America
Bloomington, IN

Cover Art by Barry L. Mason

1stBooks - rev. 04/05/04

Dedication

This Book Is Dedicated To
My Mother Claretha Who Helped Make Me The Man I Am
&
Cynthia Marie and Nereida Iliana
The Women Who Decided To Live This Journey With Me

Table of Contents

1

Preface

The feeling is painfully numbing, like a person experiences when they receive a shot of Novocain. It was a blunt trauma my soul was attempting to absorb. The transparency of my self worth has reduced my status to that of a Nomad. I thought it was my day and it was. I just had to learn not to project my feeling onto anyone else.

The thought that time would allow for clarity, understanding and appreciation of a lesson hard learned was based more in fear than faith. I was more a survivor of circumstance than accomplishment. I had somehow held up my end of the bargain. Through sickness and in health was a mantra that Cynthia and I had been living for several years. We put off any semblance of roots for our family. We lived more in the here and now because Cynthia's first bout with breast cancer created an atmosphere of uncertainty far more understandable for someone older than we. Although we had spent more than half our life together, we were children who learned to raise our children. Barely out of our teens, we should not have been looking over our shoulder trying to out run death, but that was the hand we were dealt so we played on the best that we could. The stress placed on our relationship caused by Cynthia's illness only compounded the struggle of raising our children, Lamont 6yrs.old, Curtis 2yrs.old and Ashley just months old. Cynthia was just beyond her 24th birthday and me my 25th. We had already logged nine years in a relationship and barely had the opportunity to deal with the emotional growth and change of adulthood, only to find ourselves answering questions of mortality. We had been together so long already, by high school sweetheart standards, and were not immune to all the mistakes young adults make. We had already been in and out of our relationship as we tried to find space for personal growth. Thoughts of going our separate ways and trying to make our life work for the sake of our kids seemed ridiculous. Who got custody and thoughts of child support were quickly replaced with how to survive this disease so that

2

our kids could get to know their mom; that became the priority. It kept us honest in our relationship and forced us to behave maturely with each other. We stopped looking for back doors out of the marriage and concentrated on fighting the disease, with the hope that we would have a life together. Luckily for me, my love for Cynthia never waned over the years; in fact it was stronger than it had ever been, but our relationship lacked the maturity of a couple with our level of responsibility. This led to more peaks, valleys, break ups and reconciliations then I can remember. Add in the occasional external force of meddlesome friends or family to help erode an already fragile base and all we were left with was our intense love for each other.

Somehow it seems the hardship of growing up in or on the line of poverty had already prepared me with the coping mechanisms this struggle would require of me. I convinced myself this was just another omen of life and hoped to gain strength from the weight of this new chapter in my life. I took it as a challenge to show not only my wife but the world what true love brings to the surface of a persons' being. Thank God youth has a way of keeping even the most intelligent of us ignorant of the enormity and strength of our battles of life or I probably would have crumbled a long time ago. I knew my strengths and conviction would carry me; I just didn't know that the war had more battles and sneak attacks than the obvious ones that were presented. My pride about my love for Cynthia and our kids were the crest I wore across my heart; and for all those who didn't know or doubted us over the years, to those who surmised our existence as an overextended case of puppy love gone askew, our vindication would be had.

Mom always described me as a child with an old soul, which probably explained my maturity beyond my years. Cynthia use to marvel at my level of focus, yet later complained because by the time I reached the age of 25 she would complain that I behaved as if I were 52 years old. I'd become less spontaneous and more predictable. My desire to establish myself and provide for my family came more out of fear of living an existence of poverty as I did growing up. I knew who I was and did not feel the need to conform to what society suggested I should be about. It was simple to me. I found the woman to complement my existence, loved her beyond words, and even though we had started a family before either of us was ready, I had all I could either want or need. I was on my beaten path, as the old timers would say, and would be ahead of the curve with my family and life before me. My old football mentality served me well as I forged ahead in life. The struggles which lay ahead seemed only to thicken my skin as I learned to continue to get up off the ground from the constant weight of my responsibility. Cynthia and I became like prisoners chained together by emotion. We tried several times to go our separate ways only to be yanked back to reality by our asynchronous style of love; she'd chase, I'd run; I'd chase, she'd run, only to prove to us in the end that we were meant to be whether we liked it or not. We worked so hard to gain an identity beyond that of Mr. and Mrs. We became the most independent couple we could be so that we could coexist with one another, only to learn in the end that we were of two hearts, the left and the right of a whole and what we had built was singular in our soul. In the end it was not the strength of our relationship, but the cohesiveness of knowing our roles of primary and secondary operatives in a world of struggles as we battled life as cancer survivors that defined who we were and what we became.

The silver lining, if there was one, was the lesson learned about myself. Caring for a person with a terminal illness taught me to understand who I was as a person. This led me to define my existence while appreciating the strength of my love for Cynthia. This in turn carried me. I had to constantly remind myself who the REAL ENEMY was regardless of Cynthia's behavior, which at times was disguised as that of the enemy. The lashing out at me, the berating if I forgot some detail about an appointment or a new medicine, would later be replaced with apologies, bouts of depression or episodes of flight from home. My delusion of who I was or where I stood in the scheme of Cynthia's mind was never in doubt. I loved her for better or worse because I chose to not because I had to.

In the end she only asked that I allow myself to love again. She explained to me that I owed her nothing because she made sure she got hers up front and for once in my life "to be true to myself"; if I didn't, then and only then, would she haunt my mind. She thanked me for loving her so well and told me she was ready to go because she knew I was ready in all other facets of life. We watched our late night reruns as usual and she drifted off to sleep, only to wake briefly to blink good bye.

Intro

Tell me again? Why they say love is so grand? Is it the height at which one can soar or the depth to which one can sink? I do know that its strength is superhuman so when we encounter it we can only concede. It wears the face of a chameleon, adapting to our hearts' needs. There is no set pace of the speed in which it tracks, slow and methodical or as instantaneous as the blink of an eye. It can lead a charge or ward off evil spirits. It is not a derivative of, but an exponential raised. It is what makes life of death and death of life. So I tell this story of my friend (love) as graciously as I can because she took me by the hand to experience the fruits of her land.

2

THE INVISIBLE MAN

I am the tree that fell in the forest which nobody heard. My face, carved in stoic expressions, chiseled by strength, pride and determination has muted all pleas of S.O.S.. If only I could blink maybe the crowd passing by could hear my calls of despair.

The Resume of Life

When I first set out to tell my story, the task at hand seemed simple enough. That of a young man's struggle to cope with the death of his young wife as he learned to raise three children alone. After many starts and stops at attempting to write some sort of memoir, the reality of my pain, the commitment to my children, and the lack of actual physical time made the endeavor nearly impossible. I continued to write in journals the emotional conversation my heart would have with my mind. The revelations spoke more to who I was then and what I was going through. The importance of digesting the aftermath of my identity and the resurrection of my person was required in order to sustain my being. So thanks Sonny R., Mary W., Cathy D., Marilynn M., Buella W. and Claretha R. (mom), my fellow Torch Carriers. You guys have no idea how much you've helped me to gain a better perspective for the road that lies ahead.

My title has changed over the years from Lil' Ant, after my older brother Tony, to Lil' Harv, after my dad Thomas Harvey, to Lamont, Curtis and Ashley's dad or Cynthia's husband. Even in college when I found some semblance of an identity as, "Rich" that was followed by, "the young dude with the wife and kids". The feeling of constantly being an extension of someone else seemed to just blend into who I was. After Cynthia's death my title changed again to that of The Widower. The difference was that this new title forced me to the forefront of my own life. My yeoman-like approach to life, love and responsibility did not allow me to just approach things in a business as usual manner. I would examine my own words in letters to myself, Cynthia or the kids, and the only constant was my need to understand my love, the awe at the extent or depth to which my love seemed to run for them.

The nobleness that is required to care for and maintain a genuine sense of love for a person with a terminal illness cannot be measured. It is constantly being undermined by guilt, helplessness, anxiety towards responsibility and exhaustion, both physically and mentally. The juggle of my emotion to maintain focus on my duties would wane as Cynthia would turn on me or lash out. I told myself it was the disease so that it wouldn't get the upper hand on me. The constant reminder that the disease and/or her medications were what caused her to treat me with such disdain was all I had left to hold on to during these trying times. Naturally I went inward to find answers as to why or even how I was able to hang in there. I eventually talked to a couple of people who lived through similar experiences caring for a terminal spouse, only to discover the commonness of our experiences. My hardships were not unusual or distinct. They were just personalized. The lasting effect became how we viewed life, love and sacrifice which shaped us on a higher level than we previously thought possible.

It wasn't until I allowed myself to enter a new relationship where I would develop serious feelings and emotions for another woman that I truly gained some clarity to who I was. I began to write letters to this new love, Nereida, and myself, which resulted in the uncovering of the many questions I had no answer for regarding Cynthia, love and the essence of my being. I found myself, gained clarity in life and acquired an appreciation of the strength of the human heart. It was like the old proverb, "God won't put any more on you than you can handle." Well, in my quest to make sense of my many trials and tribulations, it was my acceptance of love, the respect for it, and the request by Cynthia that I give love another chance in my life that led to the completion of my quest and a wholeness which was missing in my soul.

So my saga of struggles became a poetic celebration of the rebirth of life and love, the coexistence of two women occupying one heart and the courage to climb another mountain as my wounds healed from the first leg of my journey through life.

To the outside world I am Antonio; 42 years old, father of three, Lamont 23, Curtis 19, and Ashley, 17 years old; the grandfather to Taylor Amari, 3 years old, surrogate father to Lyndsay 14 and partner of Nereida; more than seven years removed from my lifetime membership into the Torch Carrier Club ID TC0409960242AM. I am humbled by experiences of lost and found, at how the depth of darkness has lit my pathway in life and given me strength beyond any natural human expectation, with an understanding more cerebral in application to my heart's mind. So I tell my story in the many voices I do, likening it to a person who speaks many languages and tries to morph them into one coherent language to communicate their thoughts, knowing beforehand that something will be lost in the translation or that the dialect of one voice will naturally spill over into the other. So to those readers who don't speak the language, I apologize. I've also learned that some languages don't translate well because there are no real words to capture a particular meaning. However, no matter what language is spoken, I do know that love is universal and I am grateful to have experienced it on so many levels. I pay homage to her beauty, strength of her light, and the nourishment she has fed me throughout my life as she threw herself upon my tired soul, like a shawl strategically placed on my distressed being. You can call her Cynthia, Nereida or whatever you'd like; I would recognize her face anywhere and at any time, because I am a Torch Carrier member for life.

Light Heart

I lived a long life in a short span of time; my trials and tribulations have thickened my skin like rings on a tree, so straight and narrow I've forged my beaten path. Lucid in appearance yet hypnotized by the constant onslaught of responsibility, I catch myself veering as the lines of life go from dashed to solid to dashed again. It's not that I've never loved before—quite the contrary. It's just that when my true love left me after such a short time I had to go on and accept her as a warm embrace in my heart and mind. So it was only natural that I took the fork in the road, which led to the shore where I rested my weary soul upon this boulder-type cove. As the sun set upon my life of love and the evening passed me by, I sat toes to shore with my only light being the torch of my soul.

The Invisible Man

I walk the road of life with shoulders broad and strong, cast in the image of a man. I move about the world undetected, my aura seems to make others stop and ponder or look about, like a familiar breeze cast upon their face or a familiar scent that caused laughter or a smile or two. As I brush shoulders with my fellow man, my energy may be transferred in the form of inspiration, pride or just plain old tenderness, whatever their need might be. I've even seen fear because the inevitable is about to happen and we share in the knowledge that whatever will be shall be.

The reverence in which I'm spoken of can only be described as flattering somewhat embarrassing at times. But my face is the hue of ebony so they never actually see me blush. I've taken so many blows along the road of life and even though my legs are weary there is no real end in sight. Thank God for the wells along my path filled with love. They allow me to keep on my journey, and the keepers of the wells seem more familiar to me than I to them. They always offer a sip or a ladle full depending on my appearance. They speak in simple riddles of love and love me too so I've learned to give more than I take or maybe that's the price owed for the drinks I've taken along the way.

I hope when I arrive at my destination one if not all of these kind souls might be there. I've developed a feeling of kinship I can't explain. I doubt though if there will be anyone because I've traveled this road a lifetime and have not seen my reflection in the water of the well or the eye of the beholder. My footprints can't be traced by anyone and are nowhere to be found. I've come to realize... I am The Invisible Man.

3

THE FAVOR

An Act Of Kindness Gone Askew

The Favor

It was the fall of 1977 I was starting my first year of public school and junior year of high school. I was looking forward to the change. I spent my entire academic life in parochial and preparatory schools in Jersey City, N.J., and although I would miss the challenge academically, my life had been up ended and I wanted to start over and change my identity. My father died that summer four days after my 16th birthday. My mother, who was separated from my dad about three years, already had a new beau for about a year and was in a blissful state that could only be described as embarrassing. I couldn't identify with or relate to her happiness because there was no reason for me to think of my mom as anything but mom, and the thought that she might need anything, let alone someone in her personal life, was foreign to my teen thought process.

I moved in with mom's sister, Aunt Doris, whose home is in Mt. Vernon, N.Y. My aunt's home was the unofficial family house where everyone went when they fell upon hard times or needed a change. My aunt had three kids of her own—Patricia who was a year or two older than I, Annette who was aged with me and controlled my social agenda when it came to the young ladies, and Keith, who was three years younger than I and was the little brother I never had. My grandmother Ida Lee lived on the first floor of this two-family house and was the true matriarch of the Randolph clan. She taught us to stand up and fight for ourselves and our family. She taught us to play cards and gamble, the love of Pepsi and fried baloney and ham sandwiches, how to interpret our dreams and apply them to a Big Red sheet she used to play the numbers. She was an imposing woman who stood around 5' 9" or 5' 10" with size 11 feet, which she always reminded us of if she needed to get her word across by "burying these number 11's someplace you ain't gonna like."

I was the third of my siblings to make my way to Mt. Vernon with my sister Ross and brother Tony already there over the past 18 months. Gwen, my sibling closest in age to me and I were still living in Jersey City. She became a teen parent and had her own woes going on. Ross left St. Al's in Jersey City, N.J. and graduated from Mt. Vernon High that June of 1977. My family disintegrated before my eyes that year as my dad died that July. I saw nothing left for me in Jersey so I decided Mt. Vernon would be more than just a summer retreat, it became my new home.

My cousin Annette and I were pretty close. She always looked out for me in a way no one else could. She loved me and showed pride in me like we were brother and sister instead of first cousins. She always hooked me up with her girlfriends like I was a raffle prize and the friend who seemed the coolest, she would direct me toward. She knew all of their business and always gave me the 411 on what would serve me best.

With my new change I decided to change my M.O. also, for once I would have more than just one girlfriend at a time. I was putting my shy passive persona on a train back to Jersey City. I was going to be like all the others guys and play the field because I was boring the hell out of girls my age because I was too serious and too academic for their taste.

I wanted a girl from the south side where we lived and one from the north side so the two would never meet. The only problem was Mt. Vernon had only one high school so my plan was a bust from the start. I had met some girls from the neighborhood who were cool. June who was an option but moved south; Cheryl, who I knew most her life but was young like June, 2 yrs. younger, plus I knew I needed someone closer to my age. Annette had given me the breakdown on her girls and I found myself attracted to her girl Zene` who lived only a few blocks away. She was a fashion student like Annette, very ladylike with a southern belle type of charm so I gravitated toward getting to know her. Well, I don't know what actually happened, whether she wasn't feeling me or something, but Annette told me she didn't want me going out with her. She wanted me to talk to one of her new girls who just moved to Mt. Vernon from the Bronx. Her name was Cynthia, she lived on the north side of town and she seemed cool. We met outside in front of Mt. Vernon High School and Annette did the intros. She seemed as taken by me as I with her, nada, and we just kind of stared at each other, said what's up as we both tried to accommodate my cousin's demand. Cynthia gave me her phone number and I told her I would give her a call. She was hoping I didn't but Annette's will seemed to have more strength than either of us. As Cynthia and I went through the motion of getting to know each other, we became more comfortable with each other. I became the future thorn in her parents' side as they continued to try and keep her from running back to the Bronx. I became a healthy distraction. My future in–laws, Haywood and Gertrude Stith, were extremely strict with Cynthia— no company during the school week, phone calls were limited to 10 minutes regardless of who placed them, and all time spent with boys had to be chaperoned or conducted in groups. Cynthia was the second oldest of five and the middle daughter wedged between Dinah the oldest and the brain of the siblings, Jeanne the younger cute sister, and two brothers—Bernie the note giver who always made sure I didn't stay past curfew and Ruben the little bug scientist and animal lover. This just led to more defiance by Cynthia because she was a true rebel without a cause. I had gone from some sort of loyal obligation to my cousin, to a red flag to wave in front of her parents and this kept me around in Cynthia's life. We talked often and would meet in the Chester Height Section of Mt. Vernon off from the high school and close to her Aunt Louise house where we would go visit. I began to like this girl, not for her rebellious personality but because she seemed to question things not for the sake of questioning but because she truly wanted answers. It had been five or six weeks since we started out on this journey and Cynthia had me playing a nice cat and mouse game. She told me she moved to Mt. Vernon because she was a teen mother and her parents were trying to protect her reputation. I didn't run. She told me her old boyfriend had been locked up in jail and would be getting out soon and would want her back. I didn't run. She even told me she thought she was frigid and I laughed as she tried to maintain her composure as we entered the kissing and petting stage of our relationship. She was a tease because she was "fronting" to protect her lack of knowledge and experience in the dating game. I went along with it as she gained her footing and sense of what a "Good Girl" should and shouldn't be doing.

I decided Cynthia and I had more going for us than usual teen angst so I decided to ask her to be my lady. The only problem was, she had her cousin Jennifer up from the Bronx with her and she didn't make a move without her. We hung out at the park eating Doritos, drinking sodas and smoking cigarettes. I guess she anticipated my move and was trying to block it, but I had my mind made up. So as we cut through the back of the high school field, I slowed her up and kissed and hugged her as she kind of pulled away for the chase. It was the eve of Halloween and I just blurted out, "So you gonna be my girl or what?"

She paused and said with a grin, "I don't know, Maaybee," and looked to Jennifer who shrugged her shoulders and said, "He seems pretty cool so give him a break cuz," and Cynthia smiled and laughed and said, "Ok, I'll be your girl." I was happy to be her man. I just didn't know if I should have sealed the deal with a kiss on her sweet lips or walk over and kiss Jennifer, her broker.

20

We entered into a relationship that would later prove to be everlasting, a favor that should have lasted three or four weeks at best. We found in each other a void that we both could fill. I was the guy her family thought she could never hold on to; she was the spark that was missing in my plain existence. We were not opposites who attracted the other but the complement of each other, which made for an asynchronous lifestyle that missed beats, stumbled and moved forward as best it could. Our love bound us together even when we strayed because we could not find that something we provided for each other. We had history and we could not deny it. Those early weeks of "getting to know each other" drew us closer in spirit. We did not have the luxury of burning out like most teen romances because her parents' restrictions seemed to give us strength. We prodded and tested each other, which gave insight to our hidden dreams; it became a more mature union than most 15 and 16 year olds would have. Cynthia spoon fed me her heart as she grew to believe in me and us. She was as stubborn as I and let it be known up front that she couldn't live inside a box. She needed excitement in her life, and if I wanted to be with her, I should be prepared to take the ride. She was spiritual, loved to sing and dance, and was crazy about her dad, this incredible guy who could cook, sew, and do home repairs. He was his own man, the strong and silent type. She thought somehow she found her version of him in me. We even had the same nickname, Peewee, and she took all these things as omens because I was very self-sufficient and this was something she knew and liked, while she subconsciously emulated her mom. Thanks Annette, thanks Jennifer. Damn you Annette, damn you Jennifer. I couldn't be more blessed.

4

Reality Checks

"Remember don't let Love make you weak" Claretha Richardson (Mom)

The Foe

Those were the words my mom whispered in my ear as she hugged me at my high school graduation. Odd, maybe even obscene, I thought at the time as I slowly pulled back from my mother's embrace only to find Cynthia's beautiful smile radiating right at me. I didn't question my mother at the time, and Cynthia's smile was enough to distract my irritation just long enough to accept the $100 bill my mom was pressing into my hand as she beamed her own glistening smile. Had I the presence of mind to question my mother at the time, her words of wisdom would have fallen on deaf ears. I know this to be the case now because love has been a drug, mistress, partner, foe and companion my entire life with her as primary and me as secondary as I've lived life's journey.

I use to ask myself, what is love? Like some pre-school child who wondered why the sky was blue or what heaven was like after a being told a family member had died and gone home to live with God. I was fortunate enough to have drilled in me the importance of loving myself and being proud of myself by my parents. They taught me to define myself from within first and then to complement that by my external appearance. Simply put, learn to be the man that makes the clothes and not allow the clothes to define the man. So I did, allowing the inner substance of my character to overshadow what the outside world perceived me to be or what society projected me to become. My hope was, to maintain some form of mental fortitude, in order to overcome the obstacles of life both real and imagined. I came from a home of love and discipline. I am the youngest of four siblings all spaced a year apart. I am the baby of the group who grew up to be the reluctant leader of my family. I was the sensitive one who cried when the others got whippings even though they would laugh at my dramatic behavior whenever I received mine. As far back as I could remember there seemed to be a fascination with the true meaning of love as if somehow it was missing from my soul. There was puppy love in grade school that changed as quickly as puberty and led me to believe I had a greater understanding of my hormones and this "love thing," only to learn later in life that love was not a "what" but a "whom", with roots that extended as far as the heart could measure. Had death not given me the glasses to correct my perspective, I would still be wondering who that stranger in the crowd was or better yet that it was an old friend who had changed with the seasons of life.

She was the old chameleon, who lives in the house of paradox. Had I learned my lesson sooner, I would have recognized her by her gait as she strode by as my heart felt weak. Had I taken a slower whiff of her aura as she permeated my air waves, I would have understood why I was smiling and cooing to an old tune my nose knew the beat of. Had I not worn gloves so often to maintain the sterility of my beaten path, I could have felt the change in texture of the fabric of my heart. So I listen more intently now, armed with the knowledge that she shall return and I won't be deceived by nature's eye as far as I can see.

Now I get the message my mom was trying to give me that day at my high school graduation and I've had it beaten into my heart and mind over and over again like I'm a African drum, as my heart reverberates from each lesson learned. Remember, the first lesson of love is to love thyself because if you don't, nobody else will. Well, I had that down to a science but really what she meant was that I needed to learn to love myself a little more than anyone else, not in a selfish or obnoxious way but in a way that would allow for others to gravitate toward me in a positive way. Later in life she explained that her concerns were more about what she saw regarding the way I seemed willing to sacrifice my own dreams and aspirations for what I constituted as proof of my unyielding love for Cynthia. Mom explained to me that this was truly a misguided and idealistic viewpoint on my behalf. I later realized the more natural process of love, the ebb and flow of the paradox, which seemed to act as my torch of light as I sat feet to shore before my next voyage.

Perspective

"Do it for me, do it for the kids" – "Fuck You! Fuck the Kids! This is about Me, This Is my Life"!

I am often asked how I was able to withstand the demands both physically and emotionally of caring for a wife with a terminal illness. The answer to the curious about where my strength derived from and my devotion to Cynthia came from can be explained simply as love. Everything I felt, saw or experienced during our nine-year struggle that caused my heart to shudder or my mind to panic was lessened because I knew her experience was greater physically, mentally and emotionally because she was living it. This in no way minimized what I was going through. It was understood she was primary and I was secondary in our fight, or so we thought.

I became numb emotionally to the task at hand. When we tackled problems together, we gained strength in numbers. Unfortunately, we fought our demons separately because reality has a way of making us human in our response to pressure. With projection thrown about to mask our fears and insecurities controlling our every move, life became more about personal battles of survival because we were of one heart but separate lives.

Never again would I ever ask Cynthia if I could cash in a love chit regardless of who I felt I was in the scheme of her life, because as hard as life continued to be for us she knew to love herself first. I had to accept that somehow those Jehovah's Witnesses were more than just a Saturday morning irritant ringing my doorbell and that she was not going to allow the doctors to give her a blood transfusion or so I thought.

I had put my reputation, my love for Cynthia, her love for me and her love for the kids smack dab in the middle of her spiritual conflict. "Do it for me, do it for the kids, do it for us", I pleaded with Cynthia after the doctors told us she needed a blood transfusion to help strengthen her body. Her cell counts were low and she was fighting off her current lapse from the ravages of chemo and radiation therapy. After the doctors and nurses were gone, Cynthia turned to me while my eyes were still watery but not running and responded, "Fuck You! Fuck the Kids, P! This is about Me and My Life and what I have to Do. It's my decision so let me make it and please respect whatever I decide." She called me "P" and I called her "C" but she lost me after "Fuck Me and the Kids". She had bore a hot iron through my heart. My legs were no longer wobbly and my eyes dried up quickly as my heart began to race. She slapped me silly with a harsh reality. This was not a movie of the week, and we were not acting out some scripted hospital love scene as death stood outside her door. Cynthia was a practicing Jehovah's Witness for years now, but it always seemed more like she practiced at her convenience. She was selective in her adherence to their rules. She celebrated holidays, birthdays and anniversaries with me and the kids, some of which I knew to be a "No No". I'm not sure if she was trying to keep the peace in our marriage or if she was just being half assed and less than sincere with her commitment to her faith and / or me. I believed what I wanted so I could tolerate her involvement with the religion, not really knowing what her true level of commitment was. I did support her decisions early on in our marriage as she sought to find a spiritual center. It was only after I found she was willing to sacrifice me and the kids for what she perceived to be her calling that I began to show resistance. The veil of secrecy and deceit seemed to underline her motivation as she dove deeper into her religion. There came to be a core group of friends that she could rely on who would aid her in my deception as I became more of an outsider. The more understanding I became of her need to be spiritually fulfilled, the more my marriage seemed to crumble. I felt that her spirituality came first, our family second, and this was not what we agreed upon before we married. When I learned the children were being indoctrinated into the religion behind my back, lines had been drawn. Feelings of betrayal coursed through my veins. I allowed these people into my home in good faith, fed them my food, laughed, joked and respected our differences only to learn their interest was strictly in building up their membership and my interest in joining was nil, thus making me expendable. Cynthia was living a double life and it was catching up with her. I began to pay more attention to the subtle changes. I discovered our babysitter was a Jehovah's Witness, and she helped Cynthia in teaching the kids their studies. Cynthia began ridding the kids of all toys she felt she could derive any demonic symbolism from and weddings held inside churches or outside of a Kingdom Hall she would no longer attend, that meant I went solo or not at all. I did not sign up for this life and wanted no part of it.

Cynthia waited until I went to check on the kids before she allowed the doctor and nurses to give her a blood transfusion. She had hoped that it would be done and over with before I returned, but because of the hectic nature on the hospital floor, they had not removed the near empty blood bag and IV before I returned. I did not question her change of heart or the motivating factors. She was asleep; her blood count was up and the color was returning back in her skin. The shock of her earlier outburst had left me hollow so I concentrated on the positive. Cynthia had turned a very critical corner and would be coming home in a few days if all continued to go well.

I had overplayed my hand with Cynthia and I wasn't sure which hurt more, the humiliation of thinking I mattered more than I did or accepting that I had no real control in this fight and that my role was strictly as support from a secondary position, which was much different from when I led.

5

I Can Help You If You Let Me

I know you didn't like me talking to the doctor in private the other day. It's just that I had to get a better point of reference as to your proper care. There is no burden in doing all the things I must do. The look of defeat is that of your knight in shining armor desperate to rescue you. Experience has taught me, bend if the wind is too strong, lay still and calm when the tide is high. I am your protector; I will be fine as long as we stand side by side.

31

The fact that Cynthia had been diagnosed with Stage Three Breast Cancer allowed me to put aside existing problems to focus primarily on her health. While time move forward, the emphasis on solving our inherent problems did not. I was naive to believe that all of our past problems and difficulties had disappeared because we had become stronger as a couple as we fought this battle with cancer. I was strengthened by what seemed to be a more united front against a common enemy. Cynthia and I spent so much time fighting each other for the other's attention that the reality of her disease slapped us both in the face, scolding us to grow up, or else, so we did. The divorce papers that were drawn up but never signed became an afterthought to us. The birth of my beautiful daughter Ashley had rounded out my family picture nicely with her brothers Lamont and Curtis. Only nine months removed from going our separate ways, Cynthia's pending demise made us look closely at what we really wanted and needed from each other. We were humbled and changed for life. My dedication to the marriage and my children were all I could think about. The result, no more lingering female friends to keep Cynthia "honest", my tolerance of her involvement with her religion and friends who were Jehovah's Witness became a powder keg which would eventually blow. My priorities were to give her whatever she needed, as long as she didn't bail on me and the kids. So I'd help out more around the house, even though she was at home most of the time. Cynthia desire to work outside the home fluctuated when she got bored with being a homemaker. Being in the work force alleviated some of her stress and gave her life beyond the kids and me which she desperately needed. I would extend my responsibility even more if it meant Cynthia would fight harder to stay around. This worked for a while. The anger and resentment that had led us to draw up divorce papers were a thing of the past. We became desperate to live a better life, a more loving life for ourselves and our kids.

Boy, you promise anything when there's a gun to your head, and that is what it seemed like as I was confronted with the reality that I could be a 25-year-old widower with three children aged 6 yrs., 2 yrs. and 9 months old. The promises I made to Cynthia were sincere, and I did everything I could to make them happen. What I did not realize was that my wife's life-altering experience would not lead her back into my arms like I believed it should, but instead out into the world in search of more freedom and acceptance of herself. We were both grateful that the combination of Tamoxifin, radiation treatment and radical surgery had given us a keener perspective on the frailty of life, just maybe not with each other. As we spent the ensuing years looking over our shoulders for a relapse to occur, we began to take baby steps toward building a future. We were both different for each other. I had become the man Cynthia claimed she wanted with an even more heightened level of sensibility. I was even more involved in the intimate details of the upbringing of our children. I did more than just cook dinner occasionally or take the kids out to the park. It took a while for it to dawn on me that the image of the man and the woman I was trying to please no longer existed. I was reading from a pre-1987 cancer script. We were in the early '90s and time had allowed the black clouds overhead to seem more distant. The resurfacing of old wounds that never healed undermined what I believed and hoped would have cemented a stronger base in our relationship. We were as human as one could get, although I did not return to my usual style of "checking" Cynthia as I did in the past. It would not have mattered because the light had become dimmer in her soul, and she no longer had the passion to dance with me like before. Cynthia shot her first real salvo at me that day in the hospital when she told me, "Fuck Me, Fuck the Kids," but I buried the pain of that experience so that I could maintain my own strength to care for my family. I talked to her doctors, friends, family or anyone I thought could give me a better perspective on how to deal with Cynthia's "Me-Me-Me" attitude. I could not appreciate what she must have been feeling knowing she would never see our children grow to adulthood. We talked all the time and her mortality was always at the top of our lists. We both agreed if she made it to 35 years old, then we might get lucky and she'd make it into her fifties. So she had the dubious distinction of living in the here and now, like a drunken recluse spinning out of control while I enabled, indulged and juggled the here and now, while planning for our future. My mind ping-ponged all over the place; I conceded to Cynthia's whims, as much as my mind would allow. I loved this woman, but I could not help her. Although she had won the battle with cancer, she was losing the war. The physical ailments were the least of our worries; the psychological scars were much more damning, leaving her an emotional shell of herself. Externally she was tougher than ever. Most people who saw her up to two weeks before her death hadn't realized how gravely ill she was. However, after the endless cuts on her hands from broken glasses, the bruises from falls as she lost her motor skill or after numerous take-out meals because she dropped the dinner on the floor as she tried to transfer meals from pots to plates because her arms were too weak from the removal of her lymph nodes, which left her with a drastically reduced strength and grip. I learned to dance around her frustration. I battled with myself about whether I was doing right by Cynthia while I continued to keep her secrets from others as I tried to define my role in Cynthia's life. I had a sense of pride about being able to not only stick by my wife but to love her even more than I imagined I could. The stress of keeping my family afloat became increasingly difficult. As I internalized my anguish my health began to fail me. I developed high blood pressure before I was thirty and the white hairs were popping up more and more in my beard. Cynthia shunned me more as her disease took over her mind and body. I was handicapped by the unresolved problems of our past constantly resurfacing as Cynthia battled with the possibility of her imminent demise. She questioned her existence, while she tallied up its worth. What she found was a life of stability and no adventures. I was bland and she was bored with me. Love did not heal all wounds. Cynthia later explained that she took things out on me because she knew I was the only person who cared enough to take it or put up with her. She was confident that no matter what she did she could get me to forgive her because I had proven so many times in the past how much I truly loved her, and she knew better than anybody the kind of person and man I was because she had touched my core frequently over the years to measure how far she could swim out from shore before worrying. My mother warned me not to let love make me weak. It took a series of defining moments throughout my relationship with Cynthia to understand the repercussion.

I Can Help You If You Let Me

I see you stumble as you try and raise yourself from the bed. I race to your side but you say stay. I want to help so please won't you let me? My loving arms were built especially for this kind of work, so let me use them; please don't refuse them.

I see the squint in your eyes from another migraine. How does massaging your temple turn into nagging pleas? I just wanna help if you let me.

I cleaned up the broken glass that slipped from your delicate hands. I'll replace it later with something more grand. I know it won't help, but it might if you let it.

I got your favorite music in my pouch. The kids are all packed and our journey today will be in a remote location so you can spread out on the grass. Yes, there are trees to protect you from the harsh sun and blankets and throws to keep you warm. I'm glad this helped you; thanks for letting me do so.

Don't be sorry 'cause we haven't made love in a while; my need to please you far exceeds my desire to release in you. Haven't you notice the way I touch you, hold you and caress you? I'm making love to you daily as we bond.

6

Amnesia/Transitions

Life has become a continuing saga of events I've learned to endure. The separation of my heart and mind is like that of a personal embrace of one's self, never fully extending to one's upper spine yet allowing you to touch ones sides in order to assure a response of aloneness. They call these steps transitions of life; I believe them to be periods of blurred reality, the result of the cauterized cornea of my heart's mind.

Amnesia

I recall the buckle in my knees, which was real not imagined. A burst of light that would explain the spotted visions stirring about, the tightness in my chest was more jolting, precise and exact. The murmur of my heart left its speech slurred. As my heart's mind became faint with each gasp of her dying breath, our history became distorted scattered images of highs and lows, unraveling at the rate of her pending demise. We embrace with the hope that our strength of love would somehow absorb death's blow. We were wrong. Who am I, but one half of a whole, a mind with no soul?

The First Time-Transitions

I didn't have much time to adjust to being alone before I had to experience my child's first birthday without her mom. Cynthia had passed away less than two weeks after Curtis's 12th birthday. Matter of fact, it was on his 12th birthday that he last saw his mother alive. Cynthia had been in the hospital about eight days, and she was determined to get out of the hospital so we could celebrate Curtis's birthday, but her blood counts were low and she couldn't convince the doctors that she was strong enough to come home. I brought the kids to see her. Cynthia put on her best face to convince the kids she was okay and although she was hooked up to all types of monitors she just explained the purpose of each wire running to and from her body in such a way that she alleviated their fears. She was remarkable, and she had to be because we were sending the kids to Virginia with her parents on Easter vacation and she needed them to feel okay and not worry. The boys seemed convinced, but Ashley had a lot of her mother in her, and although she was only nine years old, she needed another visit two days later before she would leave with her grandmother. Lamont and Curtis left ahead of Ashley so Cynthia sucked it up one more time and gave the performance of a lifetime. Her mom and Ashley left teary-eyed but hopeful she would be home when they returned.

She never made it back home. I immediately gave most of Cynthia's material items away to friends and family. I kept her favorite night shirt, robe, slips and jewelry, things which were intimate in nature to me. I took only a week off from work to address any and all paper work, like doctor bills, credit card bills, and thank you cards, and when the week was out I closed the door on her absence. Anything or anyone who I missed would have to deal because I wasn't.

Anything with Cynthia's handwriting I kept. I loved her handwriting. It took me back to when we were kids and she'd write her name on everything. She was a doodler and I loved the way she wrote "Cynthia Marie Richardson" long before we were man and wife. It was easy to part with most things, but her words on paper were harder to discard; it was as if I was throwing out a part of her and I couldn't.

41

Cynthia was the planner of the family so in May when Ashley's birthday rolled around I was at a loss. I relied on every resource I had, friends and family both extended and immediate. We came up with a make-up party theme and I invited 22 girls over to celebrate Ashley's 10th birthday. I had my nieces Khaliah, Danielle, Candyce and my Cousin Tasha, the older teenagers, act as make-up artists for all Ashley's friends. Lamont and Curtis handled the photography for before and after pictures. Her aunts Dinah, Ross and Gwen helped keep the young ladies corralled and her godmother Jennifer watched over protectively for any signs of trouble. Ashley's best friend Aja's mom, Daisy, stuck around as well as my friend La Wanda. Eventually people started popping by to wish Ash well and we kept things fun, crazy and hectic. Nereida tried to work the grill, but my uncle Moody took over those chores. One of Cynthia's old girlfriends who had become a good friend of mine of late, Kim, stopped by with presents for Ash and I was relieved. I had more mothers than you could shake a stick at and they were all determined to make this day special for Ash and they did. My anxiety level was high from Cynthia's absence, and my heart shuddered as I watched my sons and extended family come together to fill any void that might exist. I had made it through my first birthday as a single parent, and I was exhausted both physically and mentally and knew I had to pace my heart better because this was just my first step out on this island.

June 1996, Curtis 6th grade graduation from Traphagen Elementary School. Another milestone without Cynthia. I was fortunate that the faculty, staff and families like the Santana's and the Jenkins's helped keep Ashley and Curtis afloat as they struggled to finish out the school year. Whether it was Juan's sending me the latest pictures of captured moments in time, or my dear friend Lucille who always seemed to be near. Lucille exuded maternal love. She was the ultimate mother and friend to my family. She took care of anybody who crossed her path and the kids loved her and feared her like most people did. She would engage you with a smile and hearty laugh, hold you tight if you needed to cry, and feed you beyond belief to comfort your soul. On this already emotional day she had Cynthia's name included on the graduation program and the kids dedicated the ceremony in her honor. I cried again because I had to go it alone. My love for Cynthia and her absence caused me to swell up with emotion, as I battled the emptiness of another day we dreamed about that I had to experience without her. It was friends like Lucille who would take Cynthia to her doctor appointments to help lighten her mood, our friend Donna W. the nurse who would teach Cynthia and I how to properly use a syringe for her injections, Sonny R. who would spend his lunch hour visiting with Cynthia when her health kept her indoors or Rosi P. who would bring over bags filled with video for Cynthia to watch. These acts would remind me that I was not alone no matter how my heart felt.

I'd made it through Mother's Day and Father's Day, receiving cards and well wishes on both so I was ready in anticipation of my birthday, which happens to be on the 4th of July. I learned to be more gracious in my thanks as my friends held court. They kept me busy as they protectively watched over me. This was also the first night I spent without my kids. Alone for the first time in three months I finally had the opportunity to cry out loud; instead, I wept silently as I put my life into perspective. I made my list of wants and needs for my future. I embraced the hollowness I felt that night as I talked to Cynthia aloud. I was determined to find the strength to live like I promised her I would, another step as I transitioned my mind from that of a widower to that of a single man and single parent.

My decision to take an active role in my own life was not something I wanted to do but felt I must do. The anniversaries of significant dates and times in my life were already etched so I just had to prepare myself for the eventual changes I would go through. I was a man living in a world that catered to women. I was mommy more than daddy and it became increasingly obvious to me that people didn't recognize single fathers' wants or needs like that of the working single mother, while some just didn't get it. These steps, these transitions are what we call living life. I found them less intimidating as I took them head on. I learned to allow myself the space to garner a full scale of emotional swings, never underestimating that time expired truly made me stronger or brought me nearer to "closure". I didn't try to explain it to others. I just knew to respect my emotions because I knew that feelings aren't quantitative and I made a fool of myself every time I thought I measured myself to be further ahead in my mind.

The dreams were frequent and I was grateful for that. I couldn't wait to get the kids settled and drift off to sleep so I could meet Cynthia and tell her about my day. The only problem was that Cynthia seemed to do all the talking. I guess she finally had the upper hand on me. She would tell me about what was new in her life, her new apartment, new stereo and eventually a new friend she had met. I found myself basically at her whim. What I kept forgetting was that she was watching over me and the kids all day. Cynthia already knew what occurred during my day and only offered advice if she thought I strayed off the path we had laid out for the kids. Sometimes I'd sigh in disgust because I wanted her to know things that I was planning and could really use her take on a situation. Eventually I learned to just listen, like she had written and screamed at me so many times before. She seemed so well- adjusted to life without me and the kids; she was still in that me-me-me mode, but she didn't seem to have a shitty attitude about things. She was happy, peaceful and very loving in her delivery so it was kind of difficult to get angry at her like I did in the past. I don't know if we were on a timer or what, but regardless of the hour I went to sleep to meet her, Cynthia would somehow find a way to wrap up our conversation at exactly 3:44 A.M. leaving me with a longing I was not accustomed to. After some time I learned to adjust to the kamikaze style of cat and mouse we played with each other. I would not be seduced by her big brown eyes or her sultry lips. If she'd only touch me while I was looking the evenings would be

45

beyond anything heaven sent. I became the friend I used to be to her, not her lover or husband, just the man she had longed for and missed.

I began to use that abstract style of thinking I learned when my blood pressure would get out of control and I needed my mind to be some place else. My head would be triggered by heat building up in my ear leaving me feeling as if it was about to explode. I had to measure the pluses verses the minuses and a smiling Cynthia was better than none. I had already been in dry dock for some time due to her frailty and, though it may sound corny, my need was more about the temperament of my heart not the temperature of my gauge.

Eventually, I began to demand to be heard and she relinquished a bit. She began to visit not when I wanted her but when she wanted. So I made sure to tone down my anxiousness when we did meet. This only resulted in a higher stake of cat and mouse. One moment in particular was when I was taking a bath and she popped up from the water with one of those wet Bahamas tee shirts, like the girl in the famous Bahamas poster, Cynthia was stunning as she smiled, leaned forward and kissed me. She told me to stop trying to resist her as she ran her hand up my thigh and held me firmly in her hands. It had been a while and she literally had me where she wanted me so I conceded to her charm and she sent me on my merry way because it was 3:44 A.M. again and she had to go.

Eventually, I began to figure out ways to deal with the overlapping of my conscious and Sub-conscious thoughts as reality slowly let me in on Cynthia's dominance in my heart. Whether it was me discovering her bath oil bead in the bottom of her dresser draw, which would permeate the air every night as I drifted off to sleep, coinciding with fewer encounters or maybe merely a coincidence, the fact that I could not sleep beyond 3:44 A.M. I still can't explain so I won't. The anger, joy and frustration I felt were more about starting over again. The questions of how many times have I done this before? And why can't we just be? Constantly left me holding my head as I tried to understand what was happening to me.

Loss of Conscience

We talk, we argue, we fight, it's ok with me that we equally disagree.

The separations in our mind rest peacefully under a blanket of DAMN PRIDE!

Erased from thought, all which is held deep in our hearts.

Suspended in time by invisible wires of love undefined, with eyes sparkling and limbs weakened, we collapse from the heat of reflective glares.

Solace hides in the forest of our mind, camouflaged by trees of indiscretion and vines of self-doubt. So we cut a pathway with love slashed about, awed by the height at which resentment stands, rage covers our ears to impending warnings of danger that is near.

Untimely was your departure; naturally I'm lost without you.

The door to understanding and awareness stands before me as I lose loss of conscience.

7

Closure

Closure - The ultimate oxymoron. A polite way for others to tell you to move on

You'll Be O.K., You Just Need Closure

"Give em six months, then Fuck em. They really don't care about you anyway." CMR

My memories of Cynthia are daily, the dreams frequent, and I wouldn't have it any other way.

In the ensuing months after Cynthia died, I was comforted by the fact that she filled so much of my idle time; it was as if she had been on an extended vacation so I welcomed the end of every exhausting day because I knew she'd be waiting for me when I fell asleep. The scent of Freesia would linger in my bedroom as I lay head to pillow with her pillow tucked under my arm. My personal shrine of pictures of the kids, a picture of us from the cruise I took her on for her thirtieth birthday, and her urn placed strategically at the corner of her dresser would be the last thing I saw before I fell asleep and the first thing I saw when I woke at 3:44 A.M. every morning. I was a creature of habit and these rituals along with the strength drawn from my children carried me as I watched them struggle to live while they protected me from being lonely. Although I took only a week off from work after Cynthia died to get things in order, the respect for how she scripted her departure from funeral ceremony wants and little instructions for friends and the kids made me proud. I fully understood her need to leave this world on her terms and I was honored to help her meet most of her demands. I am thankful that after all of the struggles we had been through I had regained my respect and love for my wife. So thanks Priscilla, your consoling gave Cynthia and me the opportunity to grow up and get on a better path, which in hindsight allowed me to accomplish much and accept my current fate.

My desire to live in reality stopped me from romanticizing every encounter I had with Cynthia. I heard stories all my life about how loved ones would communicate from beyond. The importance of understanding dreams was something I learned from my grandmother Ida Lee from a very young age because Grandma played the numbers and would line up all her grandchildren before we left the house to find out what the Big Red said our dreams meant so she could put her numbers in with the local runner. So every night before I went to sleep, my bedroom would fill with Cynthia's scent. No one knew and no one had to know. I'd sometimes write in my journal the day's happenings and smile as I relished this transcendental style of aromatherapy. It was months before I discovered her bath oil beads in her junk draw where I threw my wallet every night just before I laid down, thus kicking up her scent.

I've only had two of what would be described as bad dreams or nightmares about Cynthia. Each took place in an ambulance, both with her gasping for her last breath as paramedics tried to save her life. They differed in context with Cynthia reaching out to me and calling for my help as I am pushed to the side by paramedics. I sat hunched over looking helpless with my mouth gaping as tears ran down my face. The second dream found us holding hands as we cried silently clutching each other's heart with our stares, our faces drenched in tears, dry mouthed

51

with despair. I woke up with a burning sensation in my chests as I wiped the sweat from my body, amazed by my drenched sheets.

My last moments with Cynthia actually found us alone most of the day. My emotions were running high after a very emotional day of being told over and over again by Cynthia how much she loved me. She faded in and out of lucidity, as she said last minute good byes to a small circle of loved ones. We watched late night reruns, held hands and I massaged her feet to help keep her warm because she said her body felt cold. I watched her struggled to breathe until she appeared to fall asleep. I moved from her bedside to the small couch near the bed, propped myself up facing her and stared at her until I drifted off around 2:20AM within 30 minutes nurses were surrounding Cynthia, and her eyes were perched on me. I couldn't raise myself from the chair. It was as if someone was holding me down and all I could do was watch just like in my dream. She gasped and sighed heavily with her eyes never leaving me and the hospital staff stepped back as I slowly walked over and asked meekly, "Is she gone?" They said yes. I said ok, kissed her forehead, fixed her skully cap on her head, said a prayer for her, then one for me and the kids, called her family in Virginia, my family, Jennifer, Lucille, Nereida, thanked the nurses at the front desk and went to Path Mark at 3:00 A.M. to buy some paper products because Cynthia didn't want people breaking up her glasses and plates and there were not enough in the house to accommodate the pending well wishers.

Over the years I have had the opportunity to speak with several widows and widowers. I've gained a deeper understanding of the role of a torch carrier. The morbid suggestion by some that it is better to lose someone unexpectedly rather than from a terminal illness in the end is a matter of splitting hairs. Regardless we all gain active membership into that exclusive club "The Torch Carrier" and whether we decide to be pro active in this organization by dedicating our life or parts of it to our loved one who has passed away does not measure in any way our indoctrination in it. The TC Club is a personal enlistment that the heart works out with the mind. It is the life extension of the daily departed that we must live because the world has moved on, gained closure and turned over the task to us to do right by our loved one. Torch Carriers of public figures or celebrities are not granted the anonymity like the every day man or woman, so how they utilize their opportunity to enshrine their love does not allow for the initial privacy that might be needed. The common element in all of this is that the time clock of the mind and heart are on different settings and will eventually synchronize, and this is as close as you can get to what is considered closure by the outside world. The reality is that the batteries that run these clocks are derived from the power of one's emotional capacity.

There is no such thing as closure. The emptiness, anger, loneliness, betrayal, feelings of relief and uncertainty of our new identity are just a few of the emotions that must be rationalized in order to function productively after the death of a loved one. There in lies the problem, though, because applying logic to ones emotional states does not work. Feelings have no logic, which is why we find ourselves spun around emotionally. The pressure to show the world that we have "closure" will constantly undermine our heart's mind. After over seven years as a widower, the intensity of my emotions still runs deep. This is not something I share with others because most nonmembers want no part of these conversations. Whatever the unspoken rule that applies in terms of how long a friend or family member will allow for melancholy conversations about a significant other to keep them up at night on the phone, monopolize a day out on the town, or a holiday dinner wanes. The Bell Curve is much different so we find ourselves going inward with our grief. The introduction of someone new in one's life can act as a deflector because the burden of responsibility is lifted and the here and now can be easier to digest for all concerned. However, we all know that if we are fortunate enough to become an active participant in the game of love again, it may only mask the existence of the dearly departed. We learn that we must strive for a better perspective so that the heart will allow the old emotions to peacefully coexist with the new. Some torch carriers are more successful at this than others. The ability to step out on one's own heart is difficult at best with balance being derived out of the current relationship that our heart has with our mind. Is there a price still owed? Were there unrealistic promises made? Have we regained our identity? Have we found a new identity? How am I being perceived by friends and family? What about the kids? The list goes on and on with as many splinters to the previous questions the mind has already asked.

I begged Cynthia to write me letters, which would only be opened upon her death, regarding her wishes for me and the kids but she refused. I saw a movie once where a person made a video declaration and I thought that would be a wonderful aid for me and the kids but Cynthia said no to that suggestion also. She knew I would probably watch the tape over and over again, and she wanted to be remembered in my mind not in some letter or tape. Most important she felt it was an admission that she had lost the war against cancer and she was working too hard to keep her thoughts as positive as possible. So again I conceded because she was primary and I secondary. Finally she just said to me one night as we sat on the bed, "Pee (my nickname), stop killing yourself trying to please everybody. It's not your job to help everyone understand what we are going through. Those who are around will get it and those who don't won't. You shouldn't worry so much because this is OUR LIFE. This fight is OURS and MINE. I'm confident you'll know what to do if and when the time comes so just pay attention and love me. The kids will be fine because you're a great dad and you will not have any problem finding somebody because they're already lining up. So just remember. Give everybody six months and they will reveal themselves, and if they still ain't right, Fuck 'em because these people really don't care about you anyway." This was the only night we talked in detail about what we would do if Cynthia survived this bout cancer or if she did not. Case closed.

"I'm sorry I really didn't seem to give you your due, but your ego was so large it left little room for me to breathe, but know that I love you. I truly, truly do, and thanks for loving me the way you do, and remember you owe me nothing P nothing..." CMR Declaration 4/08/96

I never allowed myself to long for Cynthia emotionally because it was more natural for me to be buried in the midst of my responsibilities to my kids. I tried to complete those last honey-do items she had left behind as I tried to shape up our new house we bought just a little more than a year before her death. The concept of being a widower had been something I had been trying to mentally get use to for nine years as I looked over my shoulder for any sign of a relapse of Cynthia's disease. As a result, I learned to miss her not for me but for the kids. This was a weight my heart could bear. My mind just told my heart that she had gone away somewhere to do her own thing like she so often did. I was used to that; my heart's perspective could digest that far better than, she had up and died on me after all the struggles she and I had been through.

Cynthia and I went through every imaginable dilemma a couple could go through, and considering we had been together since we were 15 and 16 years old respectively, we gained a great feeling of resolve. We knew hard times, because we put each other through enough over the years as we strayed in and out of each other's heart. High school pubescent passion, college coming of age, the many break ups and reconciliations, teen parenthood and the remission of her stage three breast cancer in 1987 gave us a bond beyond our youth and maturity. There existed an inherent perspective about life, love and our roles in each other's heart that no longer required materialistic stimulation. We became in tune with the loudness of a smile, the rage of each other's eye as we tried not to succumb to the humbling of her disease as it ravaged her body. Instead, it was the importance of a full body massage that only a secondary partner could give because I mapped out the trail in which the spasm traveled from her lower left calf muscle, up her thigh to her tailbone, across her lower back, up under the right shoulder blade only to rest in the base of her neck ever ready to trigger a migraine. We had lived a lifetime plus so the need for pretense became nonexistent. We became this complex, independent couple who stayed out of each other's way as we learned to understand our newly defined roles within the world of a cancer victim primary and cancer victim secondary.

8

Shadows of Love

I look into the mirror to see if you are near. I'm aware you're here because your scent permeates the air. Stop playing hide and seek because I'm too tired to play peek- a- boo. I hear you singing in the shower from me to you. You cradled me in your arms just last night. I remember, because I reached for your thigh, as I wondered how such a little woman could spoon such a big guy. When I turned to hold you, you left my mind. Shit, it's 3:44 AM. I guess we're on your time.

I never really thought about ghosts or natural phenomena on any real level, but the encounters I began to have with Cynthia lured me into another dimension that I wasn't prepared to share with the outside world. My kids had their own experiences and I would try to comfort them with hugs or talk them through their experiences of dreams about their mom. The ones that they had while they were awake usually found Cynthia wearing wings or sitting on a cloud. Cynthia also began to make her presence felt in my conscious world. I would be wakened to loving caresses in the middle of the night as she whispered in my ear. She'd sing or hum a tune in my ear, which had me pinching myself to make sure I was awake as I reached behind me to feel her body pressed up against mine. I'd try to look back or turn around and she'd shush me and say no, just relax and enjoy. I couldn't, and I'd turn around only to find she was gone. I was never afraid or "spooked" by these experiences. Quite the contrary, I welcomed them. I was having an affair of the heart, which was sweeter than anything I could want in the real world. The intensity left me charged and exhilarated, and I was happy that the sexual intimacy had returned and better yet it was initiated by her.

Shadows of Love

In the darkness of my life a shadow appears, cast behind me to caution my despair. Upon the horizon of my life begun anew it walks beside me with patience and truth. Like an Egyptian Sundial calibrated for time. The silhouette of her love reigns divine.

I walk upon a midnight star not knowing if it shines for me. Its luminous brilliance rises and falls with echoes of memories once known. As dusk sets, in the evening of despair, she walks behind me, not because she must, for she protects my back from all that is new. Reflections of my heart chambers reveal I am alone with my shadow.

It had only been months since Cynthia had died and to be honest I really didn't get this widower thing at all. Cynthia was so much a part of my life day in and day out, which is why I was oblivious to the many encounters I had with women daily as they felt me out to gauge my temperament about starting over. I still wore my wedding band. It hadn't been six months yet and any thought of another woman felt so adulterous I would dismiss it. I was having too much fun in my own secret paradise. That is until Cynthia introduced me to her new friend, which pushed me further into the friendship zone. We had talked about this before she died, so why was I so upset that she was moving on before me. She reminded me of the promise I made to her to live my life and to love again, but I was not ready so she helped get me ready. She put me out on the island by myself and said Live! The awkwardness of starting over was weird at best. I was a 34-year-old virgin who only knew how to make love to a holograph.

An inadvertent invitation to a female friend almost left me in a compromising position so I sought help from my best male friend

61

outside of my buddy Ray Brown who had become a lifer in the U.S. Air Force, Cass: Father to the Jay clan Josh, Jake, James and Joi, or Old Yeller to his wife Janet and me, and Mr. Skip or Rev. Carter to those who know him well. He politely pointed out to me that even though I was still very much married in my heart, to the outside world I was an eligible bachelor, fairly decent looking with a stable job, a home and kids well beyond the diaper stage. In essence I was a good catch on the open market so I shouldn't be surprised by the interest my free agency was presenting me.

During Cynthia's first bout with cancer, she literally picked out who she felt should succeed her in my heart. However, with her second bout of cancer, she was determined that I listen to all that she had to say. She compiled a list of all my female friends, our mutual ones and even hers; very few seemed to register a nod. She instead gave me situations that she felt I'd find myself in and suggestions on how she believed I'd react. She told me the different types of situation that would unfold for me. This would be my guide and if I was truly paying attention to what she had to say then I would know what to do. As I watched her script unfold, it was as if she had instructed these women verbatim or they were eavesdropping on our conversations. Women know women and my respect for Cynthia had been raised another notch. I just sat back and watched my life unfold before my eyes just like she predicted.

Some days I would stand outside my office building and wonder as a women walked past me, "Is this gonna be the woman I spend the rest of my life with?" I would look at women who I found attractive in the past and wondered if I should make a run at someone. As friends began to subtlety fix me up or showcase me to other friends or family members, I decided I needed to be more pro-active in my own life. I was comfortable living in my box, but determined to keep my promise to Cynthia. I didn't know what people considered an adequate time period to mourn the lost of a wife; however I was quite sure it was longer than anyone in the outside world really knew or could grasp. I came up with a five-year plan which would allow me the time to meet someone. Remarrying would be out of the question because Ashley would only be 15 or 16, and she would need me more than ever at that stage of her life. I prayed to God to allow me to meet someone not of a specific height, weight, color or shape but of a particular mindset. Someone I could laugh with because I missed the laughter and realized how important it was in my marriage. I prayed for someone with a kind heart and an air of creativity to offset my analytical and routine ways. Most importantly, I wanted someone who allowed me the freedom to be me in as many facets as possible. I saw how wearing the title of mom and wife wore Cynthia down, and I didn't ever want to find myself walking down that road again. I wanted a person who wanted me but didn't need me. I wanted a woman or the closest facsimile to one I could get. I was tired and didn't need any more drama. I had already lived a full life. I was taking names and resumes. Ready or not, here I come, world!

63

As fortune would have it, I was surrounded by a group of friends from the ball fields who protected me from getting into anything over my head (Lucille, Pat, Phyllis, Lisa, Rosie, Wanda, La Wanda, Donna and Bev). We'd hang out at the baseball or football fields and they would keep me as busy as possible. They made sure when they thought I needed to take a break that the kids were taken off of my hands and made me live a little as I regained my footing in life. My routine stayed as normal as I could keep it; the only difference was that I began to get to know some of Cynthia's friends on my own. I no longer had to just greet them at the door and speak for five minutes and be banished to my bedroom as I was instructed to before. I got to see them as more three-dimensional people not just Cynthia's old work, shopping or drinking buddies. Some I liked; some I didn't have to. I realized that it was way too soon to be thinking about starting over, but my thought process was that I would protect myself from being swayed by someone out of loneliness or depression. I knew I would be true to my plan because I wouldn't put anybody before my kids. I needed to do this for me because it was too easy for me to bury myself in my responsibilities, as Cynthia pointed out to me before she'd died. I would have to put myself out there emotionally as I worked through this process of being a single man. The complications of being a single parent actually gave me the space I needed to take it slow because my life left little room for anyone else. This also became a main criterion for any future relationships I might consider building. My children were very active in sports and other extracurricular activities so if I actually met someone and they were sincere about embarking on a relationship with me, they really needed to have a life of their own because my availability would be practically nil. This woman would require a high level of patience, a strong ear, a great deal of maturity to handle my plight, and be okay with not wanting any children down the road because my hands were full and I knew I did not want to take on any more weight. She could have children already and she had to be her own person with a spiritual base and a good sense of humor. I was not looking for a mother for my children because I was quite comfortable in my new role as mom and dad. I did want someone my kids could respect and not feel threatened by her presence.

She was the least likely of all the women I knew. Nereida was a single parent of a beautiful little girl named Lyndsay. She was one of Cynthia's one–on-one friends. They talked gardening, aromatherapy, Bible scriptures, and they helped pick each other up as Nereida tried to rediscover herself after a recent divorce, while Cynthia's was suffering from an identity crisis. This isn't what made her an unlikely candidate, but it was my relationship with her ex-husband. He had become one of the best male friends in my life. This friendship is what led to Cynthia's and my relationship with Nereida. She moved to our town of Mt. Vernon, N.Y. with her toddler in tow. Cynthia thought it would be great to befriend her since her ex was my new buddy. Nereida and Cynthia hit it off and the rest was history. Cynthia and I loved kids so Lyndsay became our second daughter and part of our family. We were able to give some support to our newfound friends and expand our friendship base. Up until Cynthia's death, my relationship with Nereida primarily came out of being supportive to aid my buddy's child. Nereida and I would talk about books or artsy-fartsy things whenever she was over at the house, but our relationship was lived through Cynthia because that's what was mandated. The main reason why I never considered Nereida as a woman I would have any interest in being involved in a relationship with was I considered her my boy's "old stuff". I never looked at her as a woman and certainly not as an option for future courtship. I recall when Cynthia and I were separated for a while Nereida was not one of my favorite people. Her influence on Cynthia became so great I felt like I was paying for her ex-husband sins. She had Cynthia pumped up in a way which seemed counterproductive to any thoughts of reconciliation I might have with my wife. Nereida and I talked a lot during those 15 months, especially since I moved to a complex across from hers. Cynthia and I began dragging her into more stuff than she probably wished to be in. All I remember was that she irritated the shit out of me during that time in my life, but her kindness and laughter always overshadowed my angst. I never had an attitude toward Nereida because I realized people bring their own baggage to the table when they try to help friends or play psychoanalyst to them. However, as Nereida and I developed our own friendship after Cynthia's death, I got to know a very different woman than the one I knew prior to the last five years. Nereida had become stronger and more definitive regarding who she had become. I felt she was still carrying a torch for her ex even though she had moved on and seemed quite happy in her current relationship. By this time my friendship with her ex was nonexistent; he had remarried and we no longer even hung together, let alone talked to one another. I introduced him to his second wife and eventually that left little room for me. My friendship with Nereida began to blossom. I could see why she and Cynthia had become so tight; she had that intangible quality that made you feel better about yourself. It was during one of our many talks about life and what we wanted for ourselves that I discovered Nereida as not just a friend, Cynthia's friend, or my buddy's ex but as this incredible woman who had found herself after years of stumbling to gain her footing of self assurance. She was refreshing and delightful to listen to. She had listened and even allowed me to cry on her shoulder many times, but she also talked to me and allowed me to listen to her. I was able to see the up side to starting over. The positive energy it made a person exude and the confidence a person feels as they put one foot in front of another. Oddly enough, this was a fine woman sitting in front of me, giggling and laughing as she told me of her passion about being able to love again. The only problem I thought, was I just found the person I might be looking for and she is clueless and in love with someone else.

9

Fork In The Road

It's 5:15 AM. I guess you're running late. Did I get our signals crossed or are you trying to tell me something I already know? There's more activity than usual going on. Maybe that's how I missed you? If I missed you I'll give you another 5 before I say goodbye.

P. S. By the way, the other day when we didn't connect, I caught the eye of someone I could not forget. I thought to myself, she seems so familiar, as our eyes kept in step. Her eyes smiled and waved hello, mine shyly said goodbye. I'm sorry, maybe that's how I missed you last time.

Fork in the Road

As I travel down the road of life, being passed by reflections of my past, I gaze in wonderment at the signs of my times; some small yet bright, others large and at times obscure. A theme of love apparent in all its neon glitter allows me to proceed transcendentally regardless of any curves in the road. With the wind of life in my face, eyes tearing from the speed at which my love has left me to go it alone, a melancholy asphalt lane with dividing lines of a love once known, I proceed unaware of oncoming construction. I slow to yield to a fork in the road. Apprehensive to this detour yet comforted by surrounding landmarks known. I am distracted long enough to enjoy the warmth from a smile, the melody of laughter and tranquility of her beauty.

I awaken from a mesmerized state only to find I am long down the road. There is no turn off and I can see my familiar signs running parallel. Hypnotized by the length of this journey I find solace in my conversation with God, as He rides shotgun, thus, assuring my safe arrival to my final destination.

What was I thinking putting myself out on a limb like this? It's been a week since I noticed the beauty that is she and she keeps on babbling about her boyfriend and how great he is at this and good he is at that. She had become one of my most trusted friends and comrades. Why should I jeopardize such a great friendship because my instincts are telling me something different? She thinks my upbeat mood is because I'm coping better at handling my loss of Cynthia. I've been crying less on her shoulder which leads her to believe maybe I'm handling things better. I'm just happy to see her for the 30 to 45 minute she can spare before she goes on to the next phase of her busy day.

What if she knew that Cynthia once suggested I make a run at her? How was I going to get her to look past our overlapping history of significant others to maybe entertain my sudden interest in getting to know her? A week ago this woman was like a sister to me. Now I can't get her off my mind. I've tried to talk to Cynthia at night but she doesn't seem interested in my dilemma, just the continuation of her newfound freedom. As long as the kids were fine, she didn't seem to care about anything else. The one-sidedness of our relationship was getting to me. I secretly pined away for Cynthia, but she wouldn't acknowledge me because she said we had to concentrate more on the platonic aspect of our love. She would show off her new world to me, tell me to go on with my life and live and would never give me her ear. I couldn't run my newfound feeling for Nereida by anyone because she wasn't friends with any of the other people I hung with and they didn't know her well enough to offer an informed opinion. I needed insight and had nowhere to go.

My attraction to Nereida was not lust that would be easy to manage. It was something much deeper and I knew it wasn't going to go away. This woman was capturing my heart and was totally unaware of it. She was at least eight of the 10 things I claimed I was looking for when I prayed to God for direction and insight to the road I needed to be on. She wasn't just trying to be there for Cynthia's husband and kids; she had taken the time to get to know me as a person. She was afraid of so much but she trudged on with life because she had to. It was her compassion that seemed so inviting. Even after all the trials and tribulations she had been through with her ex, she seemed determined to do right by him if only for the blessings it would bestow on his child. She had turned the other cheek often in life and had not become bitter as most do. She would look me in the eye and tell me what she thought, not what she thought I wanted to hear. She always stood out wherever she went because she had an engaging presence about her. That same aura also allowed her to assimilate amongst the crowd because people were drawn to it. She was someone who didn't belong but fit in anyway as she went on about life as if she did.

I couldn't believe this was the same woman who I could have strangled a couple of years ago for constantly telling Cynthia that love wasn't a good enough reason to stay in a stale, unhealthy, helter-skelter relationship with me. This was the same woman with the ugly leopard coat and strange glasses and a dancer's walk. This was the same woman who knew all there was to know about the arts and the African American Experience, yet she removed herself from her own culture at the expense of balancing Lyndsay's Latin heritage, because she was raising a bi-racial child and she knew the world would see her daughters' caramel colored skin first.

Now I had something to look forward to when I went to sleep and something to look forward to when I woke up. The only problem was I wasn't attracted to her physically. I was more thrown emotionally, and I needed to learn to deal with these surreal feelings. She could turn me on with a smile, her laugh or leave me panting with a hug or a friendly embrace. She wasn't golden brown like caramel which was my preference. I couldn't even tell what her breast size was because she had that high collar bone like most dancers developed and I assumed she was a B-size like most dancers I knew. I did know that she had incredibly big, beautiful legs because I saw her at a function as she strutted through a room of men once and they all turned on cue to the sway of her Latin hips, ass and legs.

Opportunity is what we make of a situation and somehow the euphoric ride Nereida was on was over. She had come to the realization after an evening with her man that she had hit the ceiling of her relationship and that it would not be any more than it was. Her feelings for this man had grown over the years and his for her, but she had recognized the lack of growth in the relationship. I guess all our

Antonio Richardson

conversations about life made her take a true inventory of what she thought she had and it wasn't enough. She was going to end her relationship with him and take some time to find herself.

Time to find courage; time to take a leap; this is not the best time for her but it's my opportunity so I'm gonna have to hope she understands.

10

Burden of Love

The flailing of my arms is not meant to keep you at bay. It's just the electric surge you randomly cause as you travel through my brain. I know when we last spoke you said I must relax in order for us to peacefully co-exist, but the anticipation of your voice is making me tic.

Eyes Into My Soul

As I stand before you naked from life experiences, you extend your ear to my thoughts as if somehow you had walked beside me. As I bow my head from the weight of another day, the strength of your smile manages to remove my pain.

As I spin out of control from all that surrounds me, you gently embrace me, thus allowing me to be free. It is more than just kindness, you being a child of God. It is more than your love, which at times seems boundless. I noticed it long ago as I watched you journey through life's ever challenging obstacles. I even saw it as you laughed amongst the crowd, for the eyes never lie. What am I to do? She has eyes into my soul.

Thanks for seeing me. I really need to talk to you. If you're not gonna hear me out then I'll just leave, ok? Thanks. I think I found the person I should be trying to build a relationship with, and I need you to be a friend to me now and be straight with me, ok?

Ok, P, go ahead.

Well it's Nereida and she doesn't seem to realize my interest in her is more than platonic. The things that I'm feeling are so deep inside me, so natural, it's hard to ignore. There's a feeling of fullness in me whenever

I'm with her, a child-like excitement of anticipation when I know she is coming to pick Lyndsay up. I feel a trust, the type you experience when you don't care how or when you expose something intimate or personal because that person can hold a confidence without judgment. I've been waiting to approach her, but she told me she was ending her current relationship and I feel if I sleep on her too long or till I'm ready she might be with somebody else.

P, you sure you ain't just lonely?

Yeah I'm sure.

Come here P.

Aah, uhm, oh Cynthia I love you so much. Why are you doing this to me? You told me to move forward.

I just wanted to see if you forgot how love really feels.

I never said I was in love with her.

Yeah, but you seemed to turn down that road and I'm not sure you're ready for that, if you can't handle this. Plus, it's always nice to know a girl still got it.

I'm not trying to fall in love Cynthia. I'm just taking resumes as I try to get a grip of my life.

Yeah P, but all you really know is love. Why do you think I worried so much about you and all your female friends? It wasn't that you were gonna cheat on me with some witch; it was that some witch was gonna capture your heart and that was a fight that I really didn't want to fight because I never figured out why you were so hooked on me. I had to keep you chasing me any way I could. I knew we outgrew each other, but you seemed to love me so much more after every make up it became my sick way of strengthening my hold on your heart. P, don't worry about anybody. I got your back. I'm not letting anybody up in my house to shit all over my kids or you. Trust yourself P; because that's one thing you always thought you knew. So don't change up the game now. Be true to yourself. Just give yourself an opportunity and keep your eyes and your mind open.

This friend thing with Cynthia might just work but I don't know why she feels she's gotta play with my head. It's like she wants her cake and wants to eat it too. I've been nothing but straight with her. She didn't have to get me all worked up; she's still testing me; some things never change and why do I keep thinking they will. Thanks Cynthia, for the little refresher course. I guess I'll have to come up with a way to approach Nereida without scaring her away. I'm sure she'll be fine. She counsels people all the time at work and her friends are always on her couch asking her to help them through some ordeal. This is just gonna be a little different because she's gonna have to trust me when I ask her for a kiss.

Burden of Love

The meteoric way in which you course through my veins, hurling my emotions makes me insane. Your lack of objectivity and random pangs speaks volumes for you as it renders my subjectivity inane. Stranded on so many corners of the pathways of my mind, ever anxious to see that look in your eyes; shadows, voices and noises are not your style; vivid holographic images relax in the respite of my mind.

Acceptance is not at issue; we coexist because you are still part of the living. My heart can only watch the feather-like way you float to the surface of my soul, only to take flight as the breeze from my thoughts and dreams stir about. So I carry this cross to bear with the knowledge that your weight is infinity at worst, immeasurable by any scale of logic known to man. I extend my hand to you, my comrade, friend and worthy foe, the Burden of Love.

How does one know when they're in too deep? When the door to opportunity has been closed before you could speak. I had stepped out on a limb when I found out Nereida was home alone, and I invited myself over with the pretense of making pina coladas and watching TV.

She was washing her hair and said I could come over if I didn't mind talking over the hair dryer. The element of surprise was my mode of attack because if I warned her over the telephone what the topic of conversation would be, she surely would have talked me down off the limb before I jumped feet first into this abyss.

She opened the door with a head full of wet hair as she tried to negotiate her hair around her rollers. I wish I could say she was a vision of loveliness but she wasn't. She wore an oversize neon green type shirt which was sliding off her shoulder ala flash dance. Her eyeglasses were kind of crooked, and she was at best, fashionably frumpy. She smiled and invited me in and I began to question why I was there. I was use to seeing her after work, all done up in dress suits with heels and some left over make-up. Was this the same woman who I thought might be my future? The best way to describe Nereida is a person who is in a constant state of motion. Some might call it nervous energy or hyperactivity; she is definitively a person on a mission. I talked to myself constantly so I wouldn't back out of my plan, but my nerves began to get the best of me. I began to sweat so I made small talk and asked her for a glass of water. After several glasses of water and more small talk, I decided just to come clean with her. All the while, Nereida was totally oblivious to what was going on in my mind. She did notice something was bugging me. My opening line was a disclaimer asking her to please just hear me out, not to pass judgment on me and do me this favor. If she couldn't I would understand.

"Well, for the last week I've begun to see you differently. You know, I never looked at you other than being D's old stuff, and when you told me you found it offensive, I started thinking maybe my instinct wasn't too farfetched, and I gave it a lot of thought but I realized while you were describing your wants and needs the other day that we were looking for a lot of the same things and more importantly you might be the one".

Nereida just kind of stared at me while she kept rolling her hair. This made me sweat because she knew how to listen without jumping in and interrupting. Nereida eyes never broke stride from mines so I bowed my head, sighed heavily and asked her to give me a kiss. When I looked up, she was gone. She ran out of the room and the beads were back across my forehead. I didn't know what to do so I began to drink the pina colada. I figured the two drinks I already had were not going be enough because I just scared the living shit out of one of my best friends.

She paced a little but kept her distance as I sat in the chair and she stood behind the couch with her hand on her face. There was no answer. Instead she gave me a diagnosis: Antonio, you're having transference of emotion. Do you know what that is? You miss Cynthia and it's been a couple of months and you're feeling lonely and possibly a little horny and because Cynthia and I were very close you're projecting those feelings onto me. It's quite natural since we've become closer over the last couple of months that you would turn to me or someone else you've been spending a lot of time with.

I'm not sure if my immediate response to myself was bullshit, but I know I didn't see this curve ball coming. Her response killed my high and all my fears disappeared on the spot. I can't believe she went clinical on me, is all I kept repeating to myself as I became increasingly upset. She thought I was some poor, sad, lonely widower who needed some relief. My ego kicked in right away and my rant became clear.

"Nereida, I can appreciate how you might think I'm having some transfer of emotions or something, but let me assure you that assessment is so far from the truth. I know who I am, I know why I am here, and if it was about having my physical needs met I can make a phone call and take care of that. The truth of the matter is I found myself becoming attracted to you out of the clear blue sky and because it kept happening I realized there was more to it and I had to look into it. For the record I'm not easily aroused by brushing up against a woman, but every time I hugged you good-bye last week there was a reaction. I also found myself looking forward to seeing you when you came to pick Lyndsay up in the afternoon, and I've gone over our recent conversation about what we wanted out of life and realized that the woman I was describing was sitting right in front of me, clueless that I was the man she described or too respectful to approach me out of respect for her dead friend. All I need to know is will you do it? Kiss me? That way at least I'll know if there is any chemistry".

She seemed offended by my strong position but understanding at the same time. I'm not sure, but I may have been begging, bartering and negotiating all at the same time. One thing was for sure, I had come this far, put myself out there in a most vulnerable way and I had to have closure to this awkward situation. Why I don't know, but she started toward me, sat on the couch, and said, ok if you think this will answer your curiosity. She kept upending me with her response, but I didn't care. I just knew I needed to leave there knowing I could trust my gut or should I be back in counseling for this transfer of emotion thing.

It was 4 or 5 A.M. and the shock and embarrassment left hours ago. The sun was coming up and our lips were tender, and our skin moist. The definition of her chin, the thickness of her moles above and below her mouth was old news to my fingers. The softness of her hand as it gently touched my back released a level of tension of orgasmic proportions. I had kissed this women like I'd known her my whole life; she tasted so familiar as if we were old lovers who never needed to be reacquainted, the passion quiet and intense beyond anticipation, more soothing like steam being released with a slight whistle to state the right temperature had been attained. Very few words were spoken as I walked out her front door. We both got more than we bargained for; my high was a runner's high; I couldn't speak for her, so I left hoping my gut would know what to tell my mind when they spoke later because this was some first kiss.

11

No Deposit/No Return

My appearance may not project the patience that I must exude. The walking, talking and pacing of my mind is with regard to my awe of you. So I will keep your heart in this space of mine to strengthen my soul as time goes by.

Soul Mates

It took only seconds to see, one moment to know, what takes a lifetime to learn. Two souls intertwined as one, from the roots of emotion, to the base of the physical, which extend to the spiritual branches of their being. That two can become one in a land of love, harmony and ecstasy. Duality thus becomes singular in the quest of our soul.

My memories are more like stills than reels of film. Most in order but from time to time jumbled out of sequence when life happens upon me. I've tried measuring the length of these stills and reels with the hope that I could find some correlation between my life, its worth or the order in which their vividness places them. The stack is short and the reels don't fill a can, more like a spool. I don't know if it has to do with me having a lousy memory. I know it's not from lack of importance. Maybe it was the shielding during some painful episode of my life, but the gaps are gaping and I wonder why? I believe it's because I allowed others to record my life for me with the hope that I would be around later to share it with them upon prompting. This short term memory I've relied on over the years is probably what has allowed me to forge ahead in life regardless of the weight of responsibility placed in my lap. I also recognize how I've short changed myself out of some meaningful moments of reflection for my later years if I make it. Will I feel as cheated as I do now of all the little moments that I knew Cynthia stored for us as we planned and hoped for the days when we could sit around and bask in the glow of our past hurdles? I do have my music as a point of reference, which can trigger my emotions and take me to the depths of my feelings, which will in turn remind me of where I've been in my heart's journeys. This alone or coupled with the fragments of stills is what sustains me because it keeps me honest and humble. I may not be able to recall where I was when I first heard a song or album or CD, but I do know when I listen to a song by a certain artist or hear a tune on the radio where my heart and head were at that time in my life. So when I hear Peter Brown's "Do You Wanna Get Funky With Me" or A Taste of Honey's "Boogie Oogie Oogie," I can recall Cynthia and me immersed in each other. We would dance and stare into each other's lustful eyes and we knew we couldn't wait to be alone. If "Super Woman" by Karyn White came on, I knew it was the beginning of the end for me and Cynthia because it became her anthem as she began to go into me-me-me mode. Whereas, when I licked my wounds there would be a search for Kool and The Gang's "Summer Madness". When I was on the brink of despair, Sam Cooke's "Change Is Gonna Come" would suffice. Then in1998 the release of Kenny Latimore's "Soul of a Man", became my personal anthem. It inspired me to share with others what I've been through. It gave perspective to my pain, joy, rage and sorrow, because I felt this CD encapsulated my emotional life. Even though my kids run when they see me pop out the "Kenny" CD, I have recommended it to every man I know, especially those who may need to get a grip or insight on their strife.

As I try to retrace my life's journey, I realize more and more, that it's not just my memory that I must try to trust but my perspective. When I read the different letters, sonnets and poems I've written, I recognize the truth of the emotion untainted, raw and surreal. They are the lyrics to my songs, which play out to the beat of my heart every time I read them. They take the picture to frame the mood of my struggle in a way that I can see. I know truth in the framework of my emotional self. I know that others who were there standing beside me or observing or partaking in my life may have seen it differently than I, but that doesn't matter because my heart knows what it knows and will operate accordingly. So if I got the color of the dress wrong or if we were standing in front of each other instead of sitting side by side, my recollection of my emotion has stayed consistent in its vivid detail of joy, pain, or exhilaration of said moment, field to field, frame to frame, to tell its story.

No Deposit/ No Return

How was I to know that upon your deposit of a love once known our creation of love would live life with no return? As eyes gaze upon this loving soul warm and sparkling as an ember glow. Life shall pass with time never to mold. The presence of quality pawned off in measures of random acts, which show me you see not or know.

Allowances are due to exist as they proclaim a place in the history of her New World. Time shall be your shield, as our deposits are revealed. So I live and wait on the return of said deposits.

12

Affairs Of The Mind

I'm not sure how much longer we can go on this way. I've been discreet, but I think I've been made. It's too hard to meet only at night. My need to see you and quench your mental appetite will not be denied. I'm not worried. This ain't some stalking; you always seeming to be near. No it's not my love, move forward and sleep tight my dear.

I guess some would call it daydreaming, when you find yourself out in public talking, walking amongst others, oblivious to the detail of their faces, conversations and the background sounds, which act as cue placement or alarms of pending danger or cautionary concerns. When your sub mind causes an eclipse of your cognitive mind during your awaken mind's 9 to 5 scheduled tour.

I became comfortable relying on and acting in accordance with the suggestion and direction of my subliminal companion. Whether it took the shape of Cynthia to help keep my heart in check or my father with some overdue manly advice, I could recognize the face anywhere along my mind's chambers and it didn't always disguise itself in the form of some dearly departed loved one. It was the breath or better yet the breathing as it would convey a message to me that would catch my ear. The rhythm of the conversations had a scent, which always made me know who it was.

My mind became my best confidant in my new role as a widower. I had friends of all types with tremendous ability to help me through my ordeal. However, I recognized I could not use their input toward my current situation like I had before. I was changed. I was not the same person anymore. My core had become distorted by the impact of being alone. My title had changed, and I had to find out who I truly was. The hour of the day no longer dictated when my heart would speak to me. The mind and heart would interact without guidance or prompting from me. They were on a mission and I was along for the ride. My instincts would provide me with the ability to guide myself through the day so if they appeared while in public I just ad- lib my way through whatever situation I was in. I paid attention the best I could, writing down whatever data was compiled from my new experiences. I didn't trust my memory to be true to me because it had already failed me whenever I tried to recall the more intimate details of my life gone by. I knew now that I had to be my own keeper and that I owed it to myself. It was my job, not anyone else's. The frustration of having my friends, family and children help me fill in the blanks of my life left me empty. They didn't take on the vibrancy I once knew or the panoramic effect that Cynthia's triggers induced.

I recognized that familiar feeling as my blood coursed through my body. I couldn't be sure if the combination of my nerves, alcohol, and desire were working in conjunction with one another but my gut maintained a steady eye throughout that night. My voice had become distinctly clear as I laid pen to pad to document the accounts of that evening. So I bowed to the prose of my heart as it inscribed these new memories with old familiar sounds. I decided to concede to whatever my heart and mind agreed on because my gut said so. I'd opened up this can of new film and hoped that my memory would not fail me as I embarked on this sequel to my life.

Affair of The Mind

As I lay thee down to sleep, I pray thy soul the Lord shall keep. As eyes gaze upon your great creation, a deposit of a love once known, there is a burn inside from the void left by one. Her skin glows like that of warm embers from the caress of her constant devoted aura. The caress of her hand and intoxicating scent invites me in. Take a chance my dear. I am love. Don't you recognize me? I had to change my face because it's a different time, a different place. So trust the eyes of your soul, the ears of your heart. It can be if you allow yourself to be. So don't be remiss as we talk, walk and reminisce because I only exist in the obscure.

The fear that I felt was more out of concern for the loss of a very good friend. Nereida had become a great friend over the years. She was a combination of my long lost friends. Gladys and I have been tight since our days at Pratt Institute. We'd ride the train from Brooklyn, N.Y. to the Bronx. We'd talk Philosophy and bug out on whatever we saw in our travels home. She was a fashion student and maintained a strong creative aura about herself. She found love and ran off to the Hudson, Mass. area to live in splendor with her husband Anthony. Gladys and I would talk about the latest books we read and character break downs. She has always been that friend who helps me quench the creative need or interest in my life. She exudes happiness and positive glee in a way no one else does, never boring, always leaving you with a smile. She kind of reminds me of the actress "the other" Vanessa Williams from "New

Jack City" and of "Melrose Place" fame. Then there was my friend Donna from college who, although we both shared an analytical base from our Engineering days at Pratt Institute in Brooklyn, N.Y., our connection was more spiritual. She is one of the kindest, hardest working and most beautiful people I've ever met. She looks a lot like Marion Jones, the track star, a natural beauty. She puts herself out there for people because she feels it's the right thing to do, most times remaining anonymous. It was she who literally made sure I graduated on time from college when a professor tried to fail me in a class. I held a B average in the class, but the whole class failed or damn near failed a departmental final because he did not have us properly prepared. Had the professor not told me how she spoke up for me and convinced him not to treat me like a name and a number but as a person who was real with real responsibilities, I would have spent another semester in school, incurred more expenses to my already strapped existence because I was married with two small children. Cynthia was a stay-at-home mom during this period, which made our financial situation even more strained. I never forgot that selfless act of kindness and have become an extension of her life with her husband Kyle and their son KJ. Nereida possesses these same types of traits. It was later on when I made my list of that special someone that I drew on these type of traits. The more meaningful lasting relationships that impacted my life became the foundation and I realized Nereida's compilation of the same attributes like Donna, Gladys and Tracey (the only woman who made Cynthia feel threatened because of her natural beauty, charm and down-to-earth disposition), made Nereida an obvious choice. My intent was to stay as far away from anything that resembled Cynthia for my sake as well as the other person. I had no desire to duplicate the level of intensity that I felt for my wife. I wanted the courage to try again, the strength to endure developing feelings for another woman, and the insight to know what was true to my needs as they matched up with my wants because I knew they were skewed.

My intent was to take a small step toward a new beginning only to find that the trip was much shorter than need be. I had to face Nereida for the first time with a confirmation of my heart knowing the potential for something grand was on my horizon. Dusk had not settled on my feelings for Cynthia and "closure" was nowhere in sight. Depending on where I stood on my island or how I swung my head from right to left, I could see both settings before me. I had changed her world or at least given her food for thought. Is this some kind of fluke or am I just damn lucky? I knew something was going on, though, because the fluidity of my thoughts from pen to paper had even taken on a poetic flare, which I felt had been truly lost in my mind a lifetime ago.

Nereida didn't seem to share my same level of enthusiasm when we next met. She was the picture of calm and appropriateness. Nereida did not allow herself to run with the euphoria of our last meeting. She was a divorcee who had gone through her share of roller coaster emotions as she had tried to gain her own footing on starting over. She was also only a couple of weeks removed from deciding to put her own love life in order. She was not about to let one kiss, no matter how wonderful or magical, to upend her. I wasn't prepared to plead my case, but I knew I must, because it was crystal clear to me, that she was the one, and I was prepared to lay claim to her.

I was prepared to ignore the enormous amount of baggage that embarking on a relationship with Nereida would leave at our feet. I was the former best friend of her ex husband and we worked for the same company. Nereida was one of my wife's best friends and a personal confidant to boot. She knew every angst Cynthia felt regarding me and the ugly details of our marriage. I was an open wound panting toward her, telling her eyes not to believe what she knew to be in my personal file. I hoped she would allow herself the opportunity to make up her own mind toward me as a potential beau. I'd like to believe all was not lost because in spite of all she probably heard about me she never treated me funny like some of Cynthia's other friends had done over the years. She always seemed more comfortable with making her own assessments so I hoped I had a chance.

She listened as I tried to keep the conversation leaning toward what I thought we both felt. She didn't bite at all. She was more clinical; she reminded me how only a few months had passed since my wife had died, how I sat on her couch a couple weeks ago crying like a baby about Cynthia, my possible loneliness, and most importantly how I should be giving myself the opportunity to meet other women and not try to sign and close another deal so soon. I knew she was right, but I needed her to understand what that evening had done to me. The clouds were no longer overhead, and I was not afraid of the fog swirling at my feet. I was familiar with my inner workings and no level of sorrow was going to distort my vision to what stood before me. This was not a situation either of us wanted. Yes, I could love two women at once, and yes, I'm talking love because I knew like I know the back of my hand, the mole on my leg or the pencil thin cut between my eyes at the top of my nose. My mind had been racing since we last kissed so I'd have to convince her to kiss me again and build on that. I kept telling myself I must write. I had to write it out, so I'd be prepared when I talked to her because she wasn't cracking. She's was still in friend mode and I needed her to walk down the path I was on.

The kids seemed to notice a slight change in my attitude and they huddled without me about what they thought was going on. They were already suggesting different people they thought I might want to date because they wanted a say on who they might get stuck dealing with. They would be happy if no one was ever in my personal life, but they'd noticed the attention I had been getting lately from some people and I think it scared them. We are a very open family and I've been blessed that the kids would even have the maturity to discuss the topic of me with someone other than their mom. Lamont was 15, Curt 12 and Ash 10, and each suggestion was indicative of their emotional age with Lamont choosing my most attractive friends, Curt the most buxom because he's a hugger, and Ash, my most maternal friends regardless of their marital status.

I left the poems in her mailbox hoping she would be moved emotionally, if not by words than by the gesture. I had written a trilogy about my new life and I hoped she was willing to partake in it, since she was responsible for resurrecting my soul.

The Kaleidoscope of Love

With my head bowed down, as I sit alone in a trance of reflection, wondering where life will take me. I hear a low earthy rumble; it is not frightening instead all so inviting. I realize I am not alone. The rumble becomes louder and more acute. It is the subtle tone of a melancholy laughter. As I raise my brow, I notice a light, which radiates like a beacon. My peripherals suggest I take a closer look. I turn head on into this alluring light only to be blinded by your smile. I am mesmerized by the sultriness of your beauty.

As I rise from my seat, I walk into the light with only one desire, to taste the sweetness of your lips. As I stand immersed in the light, the aroma of your essence overwhelms me; emotions and desire exhilarate my very being. So I touch you only to find my soul thunderously awakened. You know not what you have done to me. My life is no longer black and white, but that of a bright happiness. You turned up the hue in my life and I must learn to see in this world of color. My senses are not accustomed to the world of the kaleidoscope, but somehow I know you placed the settings just right so that I may venture into this New World of light.

I was beyond being concerned about exposing myself or my vulnerability. She'd seen me cry and Cynthia had told her only God knows what about my attitude and temper. The fact that I'm all thumbs can easily be explained by being this 35-year-old virgin of sorts. She'd seen my sensitive side with the kids and applauded my patience with those who seemed to push and prod me since Cynthia died. I didn't know it at the time but she had already had men write songs in her honor, capture her on film and canvas, so my letters, our trilogy had opened a crack in her heart to the possibility that I might get in. It seemed the more I moved her emotionally, the more she stepped back. It was as if I had a curse or something. Nereida didn't have the luxury of diving off the deep end like I was; she knew how shallow the water could get at low tides and was not about to leap with me. Her face never gave hints to where her head might be. Her professional training working with troubled people was really paying off for her and pissing me off. How could this woman go from being a good buddy to some sort of be all and end all to me? There were no warnings in the traditional sense. She just happened to convey her thoughts on life to me and they coincided with what I had written down and they matched. If she were a different woman, I would have thought she had woven a nice web for me to get stuck in. The only problem was that I hadn't shared my feelings with anybody, and the only person who might have had an idea was my buddy Cass because he had to push me out of the way of oncoming traffic a couple of times until I realized my new status had put me out in the middle of the road. By now everyone knew I had a 5-year plan and a 10-year plan so maybe she was just being coy, but her whole persona said otherwise. She was that independent woman I was looking for to compliment my life. My concerns about being pulled away from my kids by a woman demanding my time would not be an issue. Nereida was a single parent with an over extended schedule of her own. She had no free time, therefore any time we would have together would be stolen time for both of us. She didn't like sports so I didn't have to worry about the kids thinking she would distract me from their games while they played. Basically she had a life full and rewarding; she didn't need mine. She had me second guessing myself and that's not good. I wasn't sure if I was unraveling at the seams, but life had pushed me ahead of where I needed to be, but the challenge before me gave me purpose and I liked it. When I write it's not only at night in the dimness of my bedroom, but during the day, out in public as I ride the train on the back of Con Ed bills or on whatever I have at my disposal. She inspires me and that has to be good. I feel great and that has to be good, and most importantly I FEEL and that IS GREAT!

I'll ask her out on a date. I'll treat her like someone I just met because we truly are seeing each other for the first time as man and woman. I can't explain it so I won't and nobody can tell me otherwise.

In Sync But Not in Time

A casual conversation leads down a road, with highs of emotion never known. The crossing of our paths from friends to lovers appears to grow, a look of love, the heat of passion, a roaring laughter once again anew. Smiles reflecting a joy of bewilderment, yet calm of a serenity we never knew. The ear is patient; the heart filled with pride; we are the other individual in each other's eye. A flash from the screeching sparks of our reality causes an off beat. The light begins to dim as our hearts begin to flutter. How were we to know we would be in sync, but not in time?

She didn't seem angry or even annoyed with me like I thought she might be. My preoccupation with myself didn't enlist a change in her me-me-me attitude. She seemed more radiant than usual; her aura more sexual in nature. She had that buzz about herself as we talked amongst the crowd and we ate lunch. She had a surprise for me and I would have to wait until we got back to her place. She straddled me as I sat on the trunk of our car and the warmth of her tongue made me instantly erect. She laughed a little and smiled as she said she was just checking to see if

I still loved her. I pushed her off me and said let's go and see your surprise.

He was bald and about 6 feet tall with that R Kelly type look about him. He was standing on her balcony, motioning to her whether he should come downstairs. He did, we shook hands, stared off at each other as she introduced her new friend to me. I bit and she yanked me again. I thought I had gotten stronger if not wiser to Cynthia's game, but I never was and never will be. She knew she could turn me on even if I was determined not to be. I needed to talk to her, my friend, and she was playing games with my heart, mind and soul. Why did I put up with her behavior? She was taking advantage of my love for her. Her lack of sensitivity regarding my need to adapt to the changes in our life made me seethe. We should be able to control whom we love better than this. We should be able to turn it off at some point. Why is it limitless or infinite as if it's a part of my fiber? I stopped lying to myself a long time ago so where's the mercy, the kindness and the damn peace of mind. "I love you Cynthia and I always will, but I won't let you play with my head. Be my friend or I will just let you move on and then so will I. You can talk to the kids directly and keep me out of it and out of your life". My tantrum was embarrassing to both of us. Cynthia conceded a bit and gave me her ear. It was amazing, her transformation before my eyes. I had my answer. I hated knowing this was why I loved her so much, her compassion, her eye for detail and her ability to look me in the eye and say, P just do it because that is what you need to do. Later I wrote her a little note of apology, but she already knew what I had to say so she spooned me and rubbed my brow until I fell into a deep R.E.M. state.

13

The "Ponderance" of Love

Hi, it's me again. I saw you at the fork in the road. Your eyes said hi as mine waved and said goodbye. I'm glad we finally figured out where we knew each other from. I'm embarrassed to say but it drove me crazy, the intensity of it all. So we'll meet again. Oh, please excuse my blank stares. I hear voices and whispers but I'm all there, REALLY, REALLY don't be scared.

The Word Processor

Nereida had this way about her which drove me crazy already, feedback from her came by way of Pony Express. The more I talked, the more she listened and the longer she took to respond. She called it processing her thoughts. I wasn't sure if this was some form of cat and mouse like I played for so many years with Cynthia, a female thing or my anxious state of mind so I waited, because I had to.

I was apprehensive when I invited myself over to discuss the letters I left in her mailbox. Her voice gave no indication what her state of mind was when we spoke on the phone. Thus, my sudden confidence that I may have made a favorable impression on her quickly evaporated. I was timid in heart and mind. I was an awkward teenager out on a limb as it bent from the weight of my angst.

I never took myself to be the stalking type, but I knew she read the letters, I put it all out there and all she could respond with was that damn processing line and I was going crazy. She let me in for some reason, probably because she knew I had to go to work and figured she'd just hold her ground. I was a step ahead of her. I had already called in sick to work and wasn't leaving until I got a response.

There we sat, her on the couch and me in the corner chair, as she read the letters over and over, me demanding something, her denying me

106

answers. Our first argument found me losing the battle but winning the war. Her emotions ran from frustration to admiration as she was able to realize my determination was not some macho stance to gain position in her life, but a sincere effort at jarring the door of possibilities open to what she had openly discussed wanting for her life. I was the guy she wanted to happen upon. She just had to get past my tattered appearance of emotional energy.

She blinked and I graciously put myself between her doubts and her heart. She was awed by the power of my words; she just didn't want to own them or the baggage that came with them. I never left that night. I sat quietly in that corner all evening as the rain tapped on the window sill, and I counted the beats of our hearts, hers then mine. She never conceded her position, just her heart because she later told me she thought she fell in love with me that night as she watched me fight for our new life.

The "Ponderance" of Love

As I walk amongst the crowd with eyes reflective of your face, a breeze releases the scent of your essence upon my face. As I stand at a curbside, I notice you from afar; there's a ripple on my skin as you touch my heart. A smile appears upon my face from the warmth of the afterglow of our last long embrace. My stride is more defined with every step I take. The assurance of your love has cemented its place. Oblivious to all which surrounds me, I proceed in pursuit of a journey to ponder its truth.

I can't honestly say if I dropped the ball in other aspects of my life at this time. Probably, probably not, but my energy seemed boundless. I was going to the gym four to five times a week, working six days a week, attending all the kids' games and practice, and keeping the house pretty clean. Dinners were still cooked five days a week with Friday still being take-out night and Saturday potluck because we were at the baseball field all day. Lamont and Curt had their games and then we watched the other games when we finished ours. As Nereida processed and slowly let me in her heart, I continued to share my thoughts with her in forms of poetry as they came to me. I sent her hello messages with rhymes, antidotes and themes of possibilities on her beeper service. I later had to abandon that form of communication because the operators started asking to meet me. I turned to e-mails or anything I could think of that would put me in her mind for a second or two because her schedule was as hectic as mine. I pursued her word-by-word because our lives did not lend themselves to daily contact or meeting, and every time I spoke I seemed to take a step backwards. For once in my life my bass driven voice was more muffled as I stuttered my thoughts aloud. She had given me purpose without even knowing it. All I asked of her was to let us be and see where it took us. I would not demand anymore than she was willing or able to give me. As long as she was willing, time would take care of the rest.

Our first official date found me more concerned with covering up Nereida's assets than appreciating the fact that she was wearing a skimpy, teddy-style sundress that had everyone turning heads. She didn't get it. I found my soul mate. My head was somewhere walking along a shoreline talking until our jaws hurt. I wasn't interested in some petty, fleshy, show and tell. The more she walked, the more her hips raised her dress and the more people stared. I loved her for her mind and her content; she was incredible to converse with. I forgot we were on a date, but she didn't, and I had to catch up because at this point I was just a brother from another planet.

In retrospect I truly appreciated the delicate nature in which she allowed me to regain my footing as a man about town. My skills in wooing or winning a woman's heart were weak at best. Outside of my poems and letters to Nereida, my game was skewed. My timing and radar were so off the mark, that had she not known me as a friend she may not have given me the time of day. In this respect, the digesting was working in my favor. It was giving me the time to develop a sense of confidence that no longer existed. I could be a man in the sense of my sexuality, but I was gambling at the love table and this required skill and luck, neither of which I seemed to possess.

In the ensuing weeks I began to gain my footing as our conversations became more relaxed and Nereida began to entertain the thought of actually dating me. The scrutiny of outsiders seemed to keep her at bay, as she worked against the uncomfortable feeling of dating the husband of one of her best friends. The stares and accusations seemed to mount around us making any inroads difficult at best. So once again I turned to pen and paper because this seemed to be my best offensive move. My writing wasn't premeditated but inspired whenever I dreamed of the possibility of us together. She was regal in her delivery as she spoke, boisterous in her laughter, sensual to the touch and passionate in her heart. These were the ingredients of the woman I was looking for. She had no face, body or color, just characteristics that would put my heart at peace.

Her invitation to dinner, a home cooked meal, left me excited at another chance to be alone. No kids walking in and out of the conversation. The possibility of being a little more intimate left me crazed and anxious. I had never really eaten her cooking up until this point and only knew of a mean chili dip that she could make. She cooked more Italian than Latin but she was an enigma anyway so I went with it. She looked more Greek than Puerto Rican with her olive bronze skin. She learned to cook Italian from her aunt on Long Island where her family spent weekend retreats.

My responsibility was to bring a bottle of Chardonnay and an appetite, and she would supply the rest. I tried to maintain as calm a demeanor as possible as I prepared to get ready. The kids seemed a bit standoffish to me as they noticed my heightened sense of anticipation. They seemed to like Nereida, but I saw the walls going up quickly as I showed an interest in her as more than just a friend. As I shared my interest with others, they shared their displeasure with my decision, as did my kids, who then began to pull back from me. This was a Friday night, which was take-out and movie night, and I was about to violate family tradition to be with some woman. It was too soon for them, but this wasn't about them, it was about me. My efforts for them were tireless at best so I had to put their still faces to the back of my mind because I was trying to secure my future, not find them a replacement mom. Something I could explain later if they let me.

There was a linen tablecloth draped over a small table set up in her backyard with wine glasses, candles, flowers, napkins, fruit and an Indian summer breeze to boot. I was totally blown away. She had this romantic set up as if we were out at some fancy restaurant. Her noisy

111

neighbors played their music as she played her CD player which we hooked up to some little speakers I brought along. She told me to just relax. This was my evening, our evening. My job was to just enjoy. I was overwhelmed with embarrassment; it was so long since someone had made a fuss over me like this I wanted to cry. My gut had been right about this woman. She was special, and I knew I had to convince her to give me a chance to be in her life.

It was lost on me at the time, but the level to which she went to make this dinner possible was her response to my pleas. It had been six to eight weeks since we had first kissed, and I had learned to be patient as she processed. I learned to stay in my box so much I was afraid to step, let alone think, outside of it. I couldn't be presumptuous because it meant risking everything if I didn't play this out as she wanted.

The Cornish hen was delicious, the evening cool and breezy, her smile bright and warm. We talked and laughed lightly as the intensity built. I realized all that I thought I knew about this woman had only been a scratch on her surface. I was drawn in by our conversation of what if and if I could only be. Her dark curly locks extended past her shoulders as I noticed she was no longer looking at me as Antonio her friend but a man whom she wanted to get to know. It was the beginning of the slowly peeled removal of our friendship as we looked inside to find the lovers in each other's eyes.

We danced after dinner as we explored each other's style. Our confidence had replaced any awkwardness we thought would exist. We kissed slowly and passionately as I ran my fingers along her jaw line. It was strong and sexy, just like the moles above and below her lips. Her hand stayed on my back as she caressed it, methodically unwinding my soul. I don't remember taking many breaks. Our breathing was in rhythm as we devoured each other in the most succulent way. Somehow we stood before her bed without words as we undressed each other with silent approvals as if we had been lovers all of our lives. She was warm and smelled sweet. I just wanted to taste her over and over again as I licked the nape of her neck and ran my tongue across her collar bone and around her breast. She arched in anticipation as did I.

She found me sitting on the deck of her porch, smoking, shaky and confused. My heart was willing but my body still belonged to Cynthia so it wasn't willing. I had leaped into my future before she had let me go. The peak had turned on a dime to become a valley, and I had to look this woman in the face and admit that my mind was playing tricks on me.

14

A Rut and A Groove

It's not that I don't trust you. I'm not quite sure how I can say this. Could you just give me a rain check or a moment for some emotional clarity? It seems when you called the other day I mistook your voice for another.

Love Deferred

I had to wait. It was not too late. It was not right for these feelings to creep up at this time. Why couldn't it just be physical, which would be expected? But your touch, your smile, the grace with which you embrace me reminds me of a love once known. I can't do this right now. I need more time. If its true love, let it marinate and I'll claim it in time. I am strong of mind, body and soul yet weak in the heart. So I ask you, I beg of you to allow this love to be deferred.

Love Dilemma

My walk has become somewhat abbreviated, somehow off beat. My stance is no longer erect, more like a curl. The resonance of my delivery is seemingly faint to the ear. My smile is that of incandescent not of the electric. My heart is of a murmur. My appetite has grown intense, my desire meek. The void, which exists because of your distance, has firmly established you as a must. To say I miss you would not give justice to what is real in the scheme of your presence and place in my life. Missing you is easy; you are too great a woman not to. I hate not being able to love you; living without your sunshine makes no sense. So, I vow to keep this love I have for you noted as heaven sent.

I don't remember much else about that evening other than I kind of lost my virginity. I was 35 years old with enough experience to last me a lifetime, and I crumbled under the pressure. Nereida meant more to me than I had realized and I had ignored what my heart, Nereida, and life statistics had been trying to tell me. I was in mourning and I could not relegate the feelings that were deep inside me to some barren place. Just the other night Cynthia not only told me but showed me how powerful her hold was on me as she mounted me on the hood of the car only to leave me panting in shame. She was right, and I needed to listen more. I thought I was. The feelings that were developing for Nereida were real. I wasn't lonely, in search of somebody. I thought this out, even wrote things out. I had come to terms with my life and was well into living it out. I never strayed from conversation about Cynthia or denied my love for her. The pride that I felt for her was extreme. I just never let myself miss her for me and it was haunting me to be heard.

The tears and memorials I used to honor Cynthia were circumstantial. The body of our life together had helped shape me into the man I had become. The hard times made me tough when I had to be and sensitive when need be. I always prayed for the kids to gain strength from their loss, ignoring mine. The tightrope I was walking on had loosened. As I tried to venture out to test its strength I had slipped and fallen.

Nereida's patience and understanding helped me through the embarrassment of an evening of promise and consummation, but I knew I had taken a big step backward and didn't blame her if she retreated. My leverage was zero and I deferred to the facts—the mind was willing but the body wasn't—as I sat down with my heart in search of answers.

I was always open in my conversation with Cynthia and she with me. I thought it was great how her conversations with me maintained a consistency with me in life and death. I appreciated that she hadn't become some romanticized version of her former self when we spoke in my dreams. This kept me based in reality and I enjoyed the give and take we had when we talked.

When she saw me standing outside her place, she waved from her balcony and motioned she'd come down to me. Her friend walked out onto the balcony as she went inside the apartment to come down and meet me. He stopped her slightly, while whispering something in her ear as he nodded in my direction so I nodded back, what's up? She didn't have her usual swagger about her as she approached me. She smiled, said hey and gave me a hug. She seemed subdued so I asked if everything was all right, and she said yeah, but you don't look too good. She looked back over her shoulder, waved goodbye to him, and took my hand.

We walked away toward the park and Cynthia began to talk about our life. She talked about where our trials and tribulations of life had taken us emotionally. She reflected on the many obstacles we overcame together and how she kept her promise to me by staying with me until she knew I was ready to handle this next stage of life without her.

She reminded me of my promise to her that I would take more time for myself and wanted to know how I was doing. Her genuine concern for me caught me off guard. As we reflected on how far we had come over the last couple of years and how we communicated with a love and respect that we thought was lost. How we learned to accept the differences as we held tight to our likes. She reminded me of how well I had been handling her new relationship; even though she hadn't shared any details with me yet and had kept me at bay regarding her true feelings. She reminded me that our love was the best and worst thing that happened to her in her life and she would always be grateful for it.

There we stood, across from her place, and she just held me tightly and kissed me on the cheek and said, P I love you and you love me. That's how it's always gonna be, but you have to live your life now and so do I. Stop worrying. It's ok and I'm ok. She walked away with a small smile as I watched her disappear into her building only to reappear on her balcony. She waved goodbye with her hand around his waist. My chest was heavy so I sighed and waved back.

I sat up on the edge of my bed. It was 5 A.M. She had talked longer than usual. It was the first time she hadn't cut me short like she usually did at 3:44 A.M. and my chest was heavy but my heart was light. I read the back of her phone book to remember her words "Listen and Learn about what you THINK you know" and "when you truly know something, what's there to THINK about". I got dressed and went to the gym because I had a different type of energy and I needed someplace to put it.

Pre-approved to Love

You owe me nothing. You paid up front, so stop searching for the receipt of a debt due on a love once known. You gave me when I did not ask, provided without a clue and loved me with conditions beyond the human. It saddens me to have to say goodbye so I won't. I'll say I love you, now go and live life. I guess you're wondering how this will all end. I'll give you a hint when you relax and your mind lets me back in. Thank you for the good times; they were great. Don't forget the bad times or you'll make the same mistakes. And stop wondering about this love we share for each other; it will never end. Like folklore and history I found a place tucked safe in your heart in a private space. I will not intrude or haunt your mind but simply guide you to where you want to be. So don't be hesitant to get back on the beaten path. You've been pre-approved to love again by yours truly, the keeper of your heart, debt paid in full.

A Rut and A Groove

I examine the depth to which you've come about, intricate in an excavation of original Craftsmanship, paralleled only to the width of your contour balance. You evoke question upon question, cliché after cliché. Are you that thin line between love and hate sculpted by the rock between a hard place? As I travel through your intimate path of continuing query, you reveal yourself as I run my fingers along your walls. The echoes of your chambers speak volumes with respect to the soles of my naked feet immersed in your soil. My ears become trained to notes that are played out in a symphonic score of to be or not to be. Is this the ride of a lifetime, a journey known only through roads less traveled? My motions seem still, yet the signs of life do pass by. I smile, shudder and sometimes seek solace as I struggle to maintain the reins that I believe I control. I am not trapped, yet I can't or won't get off this ride as I sit on a hub of this rut because my soul feels melancholy and I think I'm in a groove.

15

A Humble Kind of Love

I know I didn't seem so shy as I was standing out on the corner the other day. It was quite easy though because I was looking for another. It's been a while since I've been able to relax my shoulders. I'm damn near forty and you got me feeling like a sixteen-year-old virgin.

Virtual Love

The consummation of our love had been put on ice. I had opened up my soul to this woman only to be failed by my mind and body. The ease with which she held me that evening made me search for more words to communicate how deeply she had affected me. As I lay across my bed, staring at the ceiling, Nereida and I began to speak on the phone. I asked her to close her eyes and take a trip with me. We walked along a shoreline in the dusk of evening. We talked and huddled as the breeze from the night air rippled our skin. No distraction for once, so we clung to the heat generated from each other's stare. The taste of her kisses were of a sweet melon, her scent of honeydew drawing me closer, and the dance of the tides set a mood so melancholy we could only pause and pray in thanks. We noticed that the inlet that ran perpendicular to our path had protruding from it a rock that seemed out of place. Actually it was more like a boulder of a different mortar. So we stopped as we became fascinated with this granite jewel. The onyx color shone brighter as the night wore on. The smoothness of its texture explained its life of seashore living. So we decided, like so many before us, to use this symbol to earmark the start of our new life together. We made camp beside the shelter of stone and marveled at the intensity our touch had on the other. We made love for the very first time. We used all of our senses to record the symphonic unveiling of our love. There was no harshness from sand, no onlookers we cared to see, just two lovers who had waited to validate a quiet lust of our hearts' beats.

I heard a whimper and I opened my eyes. It was Nereida crying a sigh of happiness over the telephone. I gave way to caution and the words just came out. She loved when I open up and let her in, so I did. My demeanor always became mushy and romantic whenever I talked to Nereida. I never felt embarrassed by my actions, because she received my thoughts with a smile or an embrace. She'd say, honey that was wonderful. She always used the word wonderful when she was happy but it was the sultriness of her voice when she said it that completed the connection of our exchange. I had picked a setting that I felt depicted the earthy, surreal attitude she elicited from my soul. It was the cocoon, the womb which my heart always retreated to when I thought of her so I shared it with her hoping she would enjoy the view too.

I was at a lost for words when Nereida and I next met. I spent so much time and energy convincing her that she should give me a shot at dating her that I never considered the possibility of such an ill-fated evening and how much humble pie I would have to eat. To the contrary, she was sensitive to my plight and concerned herself more with my well being. There was no sense of I told you so, just a shifting to her natural position of good friend. She had the ability to remove herself from the center of our dilemma and open her mind to my thoughts.

A deal was cut. I would leave myself open to date other women and if after one year I felt I still wanted to be with her, than we would give it a try. I thought she was nuts. What woman would ask a man to go out with and/or sleep with other women? Nereida still wasn't convinced where my head was at, but she did know that I needed to gain some emotional clarity. Dating other women would hopefully remove the stress of trying to LOVE someone so soon and or deal with such deep emotional demands. She was not looking to be some rebound girlfriend and was aware of the emotional roller coaster my heart would go through since she had gone down that road herself as a divorcee. She did concede to allow me to still get to know her, which was all I really cared about.

A Humble Kind of Love

I stand before you with my head bent down; the look on my face is not that of a frown. I dare not look at you, for hint of a trace. I sense you sense the rumble that has taken shape, the rhythm, serenely audible to your ear, yet absent from the surrounding fanfare. Quiet like a whisper yet loud to your touch, purring as I idle for your love. It is not loud or boisterous because it does not have to be. It is passive when you're aggressive because I enjoy when you lead. It is unassuming as it moves about. Knowing how fortunate we came about, it stands in the shadow knowing it's always within reach, a humble kind of love I give to thee.

Midnight Ride

Thank you for the invitation to look into the stars as the dilation of your pupils twinkled so bright. I was exhausted from another full day of chores and obligation. I did not know such meaning could be given on a personal stroll. Don't get me wrong, I've done this horse and carriage thing before. I guess it was the spring in your boogie board that made me arch so, the beauty, the enchantment, the glow of pleasures swirling in my mind as I pinch myself to explain the reality of this live fantasy. So I thank you once again for that midnight ride. The morning's come and I feel no sighs, only the lingering sensation of spasms in my thighs.

16

Thank God For Fridays

On my way out the other day I stopped by the attic because it's been quite some time since I last saw my neighbor, Mr. Stimulator. I heard a lot of commotion going on and took this as a perfect opportunity to drop in. Always inviting, Mr. Stimulator had begun his Fall cleaning. The dust build up alone made me choke. He worked patiently as he polished and oiled his tools, for he got a sneak peak at this year's Almanac. Love is in the air.

TGFF

Family take-out evening had to be expanded now that Nereida was going to give us shot. I worked six days a week. Monday thru Friday 8AM to 4PM and Sunday 1AM to 10 A.M. so the time we had free for anything personal would have to be on Fridays. Nereida worked a staggered schedule with Saturday being one of her normal days while also performing in a liturgical repertory dance group and on several church committees so her time was as limited as mine. The routine became: I had dinner with my kids and we'd watched a movie. Then I would head over to see Nereida around 9:30 pm. She'd just be getting in from rehearsals or some other event, and I would wait patiently as she showered and change into something more relaxing. Every other Friday we could be alone because Lyndsay would go visit her dad. I could see the resentment and even feel it building with my kids as I began to venture out into a world not inclusive of them.

My interest in Nereida was purely selfish I was not interested in finding my children a new mother or any facsimile of one; instead, I was only interested in finding a future life partner who I could have a meaningful relationship with. I also realized that even though my kids seemed progressive in their attitude toward me one day dating my actions should be guarded. We were all unprepared for the long journey ahead in terms of high and lows of missing Cynthia. As a precaution, I took them to the family therapist and she was amazed at how well they appeared to be adjusting. The communication in the house was tremendous between the kids and me. I slowly revealed my interest in Nereida as I saw fit. They already knew but she wasn't who they wanted for me. She was cut from a different fabric than they were accustomed. She was a working mom with a latch key child. She was not someone who would be there catering to their every whim. They actually believed that they should have a vote in who I decided to date. I didn't. My objective was clear. Whoever I wound up with had to be for me because kids grow up and move on and I've done enough sacrificing already to fill a lifetime.

I lived for Friday. They gave me a chance to get out of my mommy/daddy apron and be a grown up. We talked endlessly or at least I did. I had someone to share my thoughts with without being a burden, someone with whom I could share in their world and they in mine. We talked about books, the arts and our personal development. She was tender in her approach, a beautiful woman who left me with a permanent smile on my face. She was classy and playful, which stimulated my heart. She was confident again after rebuilding herself but fragile if you squeezed too tight. She loved that I loved all the things about her that she may not have loved. Her moles, freckles, sultry voice, thick mane of hair, her dancer's walk, strong jaw-line, piercing eyes and toothy smile, all painted a portrait enchanting to watch.

She said she appreciated how I saw her with rose-colored glasses and hoped I would be ok when they finally cleared up. I explained to her, that I not only see her with my eye's eye, but with my fingers, nose and tongue, and they all agreed on the beauty that was she. She embraced the attention I lavished on her with guarded optimism because she had seen this high before in her own travels and experience told her to walk slowly through this journey with me.

She helped me go from a fetal crawl to a full gallop as we learned we must have been lovers from another lifetime. She tapped into the base of my most sensual desires; eliciting a primal yet passionate kind of love I thought only existed in my dreams. Her love scared me because if she used it for evil instead of good, my kids could find themselves going to boarding school or living with relatives. I was prepared to give up my SSN and turn over my 401k if she asked. Thank God she never did. As I said, she had class and was content watching me unravel at her touch and her at mine.

Scent of My Woman

The presence of her aura, which surrounds my being, dangled before me, like a carrot on a stick. It's what mother warned me about, lacy and draped upon her post. Tainted linens, which intoxicate my mind, pausing only to rewind a love, a love so divine; whispers of ode de you that grace my whiskers as I smile on cue. Raptures of delight elevate my senses to erotic heights. I tasted your familiar flavor in my dreams last night only to awaken, aroused with an abundant appetite. I know not what I do; I know not who I am, as I follow in pursuit of the scent of my woman.

She left me in a constant state of flux and I couldn't contain it from the outside world. My friends soon learned I was no longer available for late night card parties or anything else for that matter. I had found a little slice of heaven and I wouldn't trade it for the world.

If Cynthia was the love of my life, then Nereida has to be what they call my Soul Mate. The natural way in which her love permeates my blood is slow and intense. There is nothing forced or contrived in how we love. The passion takes us on a journey of each other's desires, never stopping until we reach some unwritten height of climax. It is mature and sophisticated as need be or as basic as our urges require. We have completed the other's need to love left unfinished by past loves.

133

Starving Souls

It's been some time since we last met, maybe only seconds since time has ticked as I move from breast to breast. The longing felt between the breaths as I pant so erect. I see a look; I hear your request as I paint the canvas of your body with sweeping caresses. Pupils dilated upon the spreading of your wings, you feed me appetite suppressants of raspberries and nectar cuisine. Growling echoes of lust scream from my loins of hunger, which only you can satisfy. Feed me on a hot bed of passionate delight, thighs full of thick thunderous requite, a back arched in the sweat of anticipation, an ass full moon of invitation. I am famished and hoarse of thirst as my soul screams because I'm starving for your love.

I now live in a world of virtual recall as the slightest thing causes the replay of the previous Friday's event. It's like I have built in HBO of our last night of love, and it sustains me until the next week when we air a new episode. Each episode is an original picking up where the last one ended. It's a made for an adult audience so I try to guard myself and retreat somewhere private so I can take it all in.

Rendezvous of Dé já Vu

I see, I see, you see, we see to meet our hearts to be. A wave of your tongue, jasmine hints about your neck, I press my flesh upon request.

That of a caress so exciting and new, wait a minute my body knows this tune. That explains free falling euphoria raining down so soon. Oops Ah SH__ I'm drenched as we happen upon dé já vu of a rendezvous.

17

The Cola Wars
Pepsi -vs. - Coke

As I sit on my island all alone, this lovely hamlet I do adore. This inlet allows for the most spectacular view, from which I can see more than most; that do what I do.

137

THE COLA WARS

Pepsi -vs. - Coke

I was never the player type when it came to women, although I did play from time to time. My preference has always been love, because of the fullness it makes me feel emotionally. I like being in love and need love to truly connect with a woman. I knew if I didn't convince Nereida that I had grown she wouldn't give us any real consideration, so I did. My interest in Nereida literally forced me on the market. I could have gone on indefinitely by myself, but my gut told me she was the one, so as instructed, I began taking resumes. I left myself open to any and every woman as I gauged my equilibrium as a single man.

Nereida was right and so was I. I did need to meet other women and I did. I proceeded to engage my thoughts on women in the most basic of circumstances. I appealed to any physical, mental or cosmic attraction I felt as I sorted my life out. Weeks turned to months and my feelings were full blown for Nereida, but I had to keep them in a box. I still wrote her poems and love notes to remind her of the depth to which my feelings for her had grown. The problem was that the more I dated other women, the more I knew she was the one. I was determined to give her what she wanted so I let her know of the dates and rendezvous I went on. I was angry at her for putting me through this, even though I knew she was right. I had forgotten the flip side of love—how frustrating it could be.

I was in control of my life but not my heart. I had given it freely to Nereida and she was slowly and graciously accepting it. She stepped cautiously beside me as we fell in love with one another. The nay sayers stared, talked, and denounced what they couldn't understand, and I didn't care, although she did. She had to. I hated the glare our relationship had placed her under. The kids had become reserved and sometimes cold to her. I was pushing a boulder up a hill and I had barely gotten my legs back. So I relied on my determination to succeed. My confidence was back and I owed nobody so I carried on for me. I constantly reminded myself of Cynthia's words', "YOU OWE ME NOTHING and LIVE YOUR LIFE". If she was ok with it, then the rest of the world would have to be. Cynthia had given me a clean slate, free of any guilt and I realized I owed any future happiness to this selfless act. I had to put to rest many of the residual problems that Cynthia had left me to clean up, both personally and financially, and ignore her motivation for wiping the slate clean. We were partners. She did her part so I had to let things go in order to do mine.

There became a familiar pattern developing in our relationship. Something or someone would cause Nereida to walk away from the relationship. As her feelings began to grow, the uncertainty of whether the stress of outside forces was worth it, would make her run. So I chased her like I knew how, because this is what I did throughout my relationship with my wife. Finally she gave me an ultimatum of sorts. She was tired of sharing me and was ready for us to go solo. I wasn't and my stubborn pride told me not to agree. I was the one who asked for an exclusive relationship, but she said no. Now she was dictating to me to stop what she started. So I let her go as I continued to explore who or what I wanted. She went on with her life and I with mine. We were hollow by the time we parted, neither gaining the leverage we were looking to gain from the other.

I began to sort through the "transfer of emotion" that kept creeping out of me. I had told myself that I made peace with my past and the demons from the unresolved issues from my marriage, but I had not. I wasn't sure if I was trying to protect myself from making the same mistake my mother warned me about long ago by letting love make me weak or was Nereida being heaped onto a pile with Cynthia because she held my heart. I was thankful that I had met a woman who displayed the patience to stand by me as I rehabilitated my mind, body and soul, but I had to establish myself in the relationship or I would find myself sacrificing my wants and needs again only to watch history repeat itself.

I became Marker because I kept indicators, chits or whatever to indicate the path I was traveling as I learned to deal with my feelings for Nereida, to guard against chasing my tail. She became Heap because that was how I began to make her feel as she felt the comparison between her and Cynthia continued to grow. We had known the other's long lost love as intimate friends so we had built in knowledge of the scars of each other's heart. Sometimes it helped; most times it did not. We were both very different because of our losses but we found ourselves measuring each other instead of developing the trust for the basis of any relationship.

I had a favorite expression I used to say to Cynthia when we were on the outs and she'd tell me to go find somebody else. I would tell her "just because I love Pepsi doesn't mean I won't drink Coke". When Cynthia was at the end of her rope she'd push me away or challenge me to see if I would run and turn to another woman. When we were younger, I did, not because she lacked anything. I did it because? I had no answers then and I have none twenty years later. I couldn't understand how a woman who had a man who was dedicated to her, provided for her and their kids, loved her more than he loved himself, how could she constantly treat him as an afterthought. It wasn't until Cynthia was near death that she finally explained herself to me; unfortunately, by then her feelings were buried under years of pain and suffering as were mine. I wasn't about to repeat these patterns with Nereida so I drank Coke, Dr. Pepper, RC Cola, whatever beverage that was being served. I would return to her when I knew I had no need to be anywhere else, which would give her the confidence to build a future with me, if she was still around. I left her with food for thought with the hope that I'd have a chance at some later time. Our chemistry was incredible, as if we'd known each other a lifetime. As she trusted me, her unbridled passion raised the bar on the height of our love.

I watched her date other men as I panicked internally that she might meet Mr. Right. We were in the friend zone and I hated it. It didn't matter how wonderfully another woman would treat me, Nereida had my heart so they never really stood a chance and time was making it very obvious. She missed me too but the issue at hand was no longer if we could love each other, but were we willing to take the next step. We had already experienced so many wonderful milestones over the last year and a half, but I hadn't figured out how to stop her from running. She was an independent woman who knew what she wanted and didn't apologize or make excuses for it. She humbled me without taunting, which made me respect her dignity even more. I needed a plan to get her back without losing face. I loved Pepsi and I was tired of drinking Coke. So I wrote her a little story.

Hello from an old friend: Heap

I know it's been a while since we last talked. It's not that you haven't been on my mind, matter of fact you've been all that I think about as I walk these lonely shorelines wondering how much longer till we can meet again, hold each others hand, exchange stares, laughs and have pleasant conversation. The breeze seems still, the view cloudy, without the light you so generously emit from your smile. I took a walk into town today and stopped at my favorite fruit stand to pick up a bushel of berries and a few melons. I was quite lucky to still get such a succulent harvest this time of year. The owner explained that he met a stranger who gave him some concoction that he could spray on the fruit to aid them in being so plump and juicy. Who was this person I asked? He said he only knows she goes by the name of Iliana, and he believes she may be Greek or of Mediterranean decent. I could only smile for I knew my goddess had found yet another way to cross my path and lift my spirit. So, allow me to retreat to my rock, where I shall wait because I will soon enjoy the nectar of my desire.

18

Soul Of A Man

The trunk of a man's heart, lined with fortitude, filled with experience, maintaining a capacity of nth cubic depth measured exponentially by his inner awareness with its weight calibrated in degrees of self worth.

Antonio Richardson

Fetal Reaction

As I lay, head to toe, crumbled body, flesh tightened and exhausted from another marathon of my daily grind, the indentation of my weight across my mattress seems to press hard against the slats that try to support me. As her hand swept between each blade of my back, as she counted each joint of my vertebrae, circular in motion, pendulous in rhythm, the growl of my breath began to subside from murmurs to coos. She was subtle and smooth. She had gone fetal on me to relax my mood.

I led her down my hidden path, cornered her with kisses, some soft, some wet, most deep inside, probing never allowing her to gain control of her breath, as I raised the stakes of passion I knew I could brew. She twitched in exhilaration, arched with some convulsions as her pores began to release the scent of victory. She exalted herself to where I wanted her to be. She had taken the reins or I gave them to her. I wasn't sure. Is the cart before the horse or not? I don't know, but I knew as she smiled that I was the horse as she rode me lap after lap around the track. I was a stallion placed in a harness as I strained to get the carrot at the end of her stick. She contracted her muscles as she led me across the finish line, relaxing them in victory as we panted about in our bodies' sweat. My gallop less defined, humbled by how she turned on a dime; she had done it again and left me FETAL.

146

Soul of A Man

It was time for a little humiliation on my part. I had won her heart, which I thought would be the crowning jewel for my future. She taught me how to love again and I taught her to be stronger as a person. We complemented each other better than we ever imagined, her an independent woman and me a self-sufficient man. Our egos had to learn to coexist in order for us to be. She always said I had met my match when it came to her being my woman. I partially agreed because she matched me blow for blow when it came to love. We were two givers who had to learn to take cues on taking what was rightfully ours.

I always relied on my music to help set a mood, to lift me up, or take me on an emotional ride. My solace was found by repeatedly listening to the Kenny Latimore CD titled "Soul of a Man." A good friend and fellow Torch Carrier named Marilynn turned me onto it and I couldn't turn it off. Marilynn and I spent endless hours on the phone, hanging out while talking about our plights. She lost her husband the same year I lost Cynthia. She had a son Marshall who played ball with my son Curt, and they were constantly mistaken for each other because they were the two dark-skinned kids. Her daughter La Shawna was friends with my son Lamont so our families became extensions of each other as we exchanged surrogate roles to our children. We were lucky because we had each other and didn't have to burden our other friends with

147

discussion about our lost loves. We were war buddies who fought the same fight to live.

Kenny, as we called him, told our story of emotional highs, lows and feelings of uncertainty, which would leave us feeling like we just left a church sermon. I found in one album my life story and I wished he had arrived two years earlier. I no longer shuffled through racks of CDs to find a handful of songs to ease my pain. Kenny helped me talk to Cynthia, Nereida, my kids and God in 90 minutes. He made me laugh at my pain as he exhilarated my spirit. He gave me courage when I needed to step and bought to focus where I wanted to be.

My life had settled into a rhythm that was tight and routine. I had as much control as I could with respect to the everyday occurrence at the kids' school, work, games and extra curricular activities the kids involved themselves in. I learned from the lessons of my past, but I found myself backsliding with my attitude. I had established a path for my five-year plan. I just needed to sure up Nereida to make it happen. I was at peace with myself so Cynthia didn't have to lecture me as much in my dreams. We became friends like she wanted, and I valued her input when she gave it. I was in a mellow state of mind these days, and my stride was defined. My children had settled into being kids of a single parent. They gave me the usual headaches that teenagers give their parents. I was fighting with Lamont to get him to focus more on his studies so he would be prepared for college, though his interest was practically nil. He was a fantastic baseball player and knew he needed to go to college to prolong his career. Curt was still a three-sport star playing football, basketball and baseball at a private school in Rye New York while Ashley began to show more interest in sports as she continued her cheerleading and dance locally. Ashley also developed a newfound interest in field hockey at RCDS while living in Curtis' shadow.

I continued to write but without the same frequency as before. I missed writing but stopped making time for it. The motivation was gone because the inspiration and encouragement were no longer a part of my day-to-day existence. So I put my mind back where it belonged.

No Clichés

There are no clichés that come to mind when trying to describe the beauty that is you. There is no ode of or ode to that can quite capture my melancholy mood. There are no stories, which I have read of late that can compare with that which we have written. So as I sit and wait anxious to see your smiling face, I'm held by the comfort of our last embrace.

My absence in and out of Nereida's life began to place me back in the heap pile. I was determined not to pay for the sins of another and I knew she shouldn't either. We had a full-blown relationship going with all the problems that exist. Our lifestyle gave us all the space we needed, but the honeymoon was long over and we had to put work in to make it right. I began to visit her one or two days during the week just to put more time in because that's what we needed. We were strong, but Friday nights out were not enough. Nereida demanded that I take better care of myself and rest more when I could. She began to speak up and behave more like my lady, and it made me feel good. She became hands on in the relationship and challenged me as I use to challenge her. She had more backbone in her tone and took me up on pleas to speak what was truly in her heart.

When I pushed too hard for her attention, she would shut down. When I initially set out to find someone, one of the top traits I was looking for in a woman was someone who had her own life. Now I found myself resentful of Nereida's busy schedule. I couldn't or wouldn't ask her to give up her involvement with her liturgical dance group, because that was her outlet and passion to balance her life emotionally. Her involvement with her church gave her the spiritual base necessary to live her life. There was no time for me and I hated her for it. She no longer put herself out there for other men. She said she loved me and had no desire for anyone else. I got what I prayed for. I just had to learn to embrace it. I wrote her a series of poems, which vented my frustration at where I found myself because I no longer operated in the negative realm as I did in my marriage. This doesn't suggest that we didn't argue from time to time because we did. It's just that I knew she could hear me better when I spoke on paper and I had reference to my claims.

I'm Sorry I'm Not Like Most

When I kissed you on the lips and sighed at the warmth of your tongue, I'm sorry I enjoyed it, well I'm not like most.

When you rolled over into my arms after a passionate night of love, I embraced and cherished our moment of glow, so I apologize. You see, I'm not like most.

When you told me about your tired heart, body and soul, I caressed your spirit. Please excuse me, but I'm not like most.

When you dreamed of being loved for your content and contribution to life, as we know it, I fell upon bent knee in relief. You see, I'm funny that way because I'm not like most.

As you arched your back and protruded your breasts with screams of I am woman hear me roar, I held hand to ear without angst or fear.

Fantasies of you and me, romance and dreams to be an invitation to life shared as one, instead of night delights with quick exit flights.

Side to side, out in front, with faith at our back, protected, hands instinctively intertwined as we gaze in the mirrors of each others' eyes. YOU NOW SEE, I'M NOT LIKE MOST.

19

The Deal

My presence can not be defined by the length of my vine. Time sculpts my face with nature's grace. So as others look up toward the sky and get caught up in the bloom, remember the strength of this fossil, my symbol to you.

The Deal

I had come to terms with who I was and was ready to take a firmer grip on my relationship with Nereida. Some friends applauded my relationship with Nereida because they saw how happy I was when we were together; others cautioned me that I needed to establish her more in my everyday life with the kids if I was as serious about her as I professed. My plan was simple. I would concede to whatever we agreed upon if it meant we would BE TOGETHER. I was not offering a ring or a marriage proposal because it would be in direct conflict of what I had laid out for me and the kids. However, I would give her anything else if she understood my decision about not looking to get married.

Nereida understood what I was looking to achieve and respected my need to do right by my kids so marriage was not the real issue for her. She could be patient but she wanted no part in a long-term dating situation that could lead to nowhere. She knew I loved her and that was not her concern. She wanted to know what my five and ten-year plan was for Nereida and Antonio. Was she going to look up and find herself fifty years old and still dating? This was not an attractive proposition for her. She wanted a commitment of fidelity, the inclusion in all aspects of my life and equal billing in the planning of our future.

We talked for nearly two hours back and forth as we examined the level of sincerity in each other's eyes. I explained to her that I was tired of pretending that there was someone else for me. I knew from that first night we kissed, but I went out and lived life as she suggested and found myself at the same place I started, more seasoned but with the same hunger for an opportunity at a life with her. I put it all out there and exposed every pore of my emotion to her that day, and as the kids went on about their life, as we sat on my couch, she looked about us and conceded to take my hand for the final time. She promised me she wouldn't run from me if things got tough. We promised each other the love we were both waiting for. We allowed our souls to embark on the kinship they had longed for, and we became a couple who would only look back to reflect on the promise of a future.

I reminded her of the rock I spoke of the night I made love to her on the phone. That black, somewhat out of place granite, which gleamed as the others faded under the night's glare. How its composition allowed it to shine distinctly as the polishing of the water cast upon it. That symbol would represent me and was indicative of what I would represent in the scheme of her life. Something she could perch her soul on. Something she could touch to feel the smoothness of my centered mind, or just marvel at, as she anticipates time well-spent learning its history. I had taken her mind to somewhere familiar and good. I reminded her of my strengths and how she enjoyed the freedom of being a woman who did not have to prop me or my ego up in order to please me. I spoke about the diverse ways I expressed my love to her and how it unleashed the woman she had been searching for all these years. I was confident but not cocky this day. She saw the passion and determination as I spoke and she conceded. We closed the deal with a small kiss and a strong embrace. We exhaled because we no longer had to live without a purpose. We would lay brick to our foundation and would build a home for our hearts.

Rocks Have Roots Too

I sit before you a rock upon your beach, planted firmly within your sands. As high tides douse my face in exhilaration, low tides erode the land beneath. Simple in my appearance sometimes mistaken for stoic, often sat upon, leaned on and jumped from. I'm sometimes even moved an inch or two. Nature's ever-changing mood leaves you with concern. Will my favorite rock be washed away by a current, swallowed up by a dune, taken away by some other means? Fear not, for a rock this old must have roots.

20

The Blessing
Want / Need

I'm sorry that in our most trying times I've deferred to someone else's word to bring into focus how I feel. There is so much more that needs to be said. As I stand strong because I must, I draw strength from what you have shown me. I will allow the visual to inspire me and embrace with pride the grace in which you have loved me. My sunshine, my only sunshine, please don't ever go away.

The Blessing

The days turned into weeks, the weeks into months, and months into years. Cynthia no longer felt the need to speak to me nightly as she did early on when she left me. She has taken a more active presence in my daily endeavors, as a passive observer, more like a sidekick who encourages me on. I am amazed at the grace with which she interacts with me, supportive in the decisions I have made. There have been times when she questioned my commitment to Nereida, occasionally testing me by telling me she wanted back in my life.

The first time she tried to test me Cynthia was blunt. She stopped by while Nereida was over but happened to be taking a shower. She didn't try to be discreet or whisper her intention. She just stated her position. She was tired and was ready to come home. I was completely thrown because she seemed quite happy with her new life. There was no mention of the kids, of how much she missed them, or how they needed her; it was directed squarely at me. I love you, you love me and it's time for me to be home with you. I back pedaled a little as I looked toward the bathroom. I had learned not to react quickly to Cynthia's requests because she would hold me to them with her stares. I became defensive and spun the situation around. I questioned her motive and her timing. I reminded her that our lives were never about love and how dare she try to play me like a puppet and just expect me to give her whatever she wanted. She smiled and kissed me and said she'd be back and left. I wasn't sure what to say to Nereida so I said nothing because she once told me early on that she knew she'd always live in the shadow of Cynthia.

Cynthia sent advocates to tell me to pick her up at the airport once, she'd be on an incoming flight but I didn't show. I knew how much I loved her, but I wasn't about to play her games or be positioned. I couldn't risk getting my hopes up only to have her change her mind and leave me again. I've always respected the love I have for Cynthia, but I knew I had to hold my ground. My life was with Nereida now and I was determined to make a go of it. I never believed in trading in one person for another, and Cynthia was fully aware of this from my own personal digressions. She knew she was the exception to all my rules and she was calling in her chits. So I held pat until she recognized I was serious.

She never seemed bitter by my stance, just more determined in testing my heart. She was okay with me loving Nereida, but she wanted to know if I was just being desperate to regain something I thought I had or was I going to be true to my word. I kept forgetting that Cynthia and Nereida were extremely close. She was her GIRL who kept her sane. That's when it dawned on me. She wasn't interested in getting back with me; she was looking out for her old partner.

Nereida was that one person who Cynthia use to turn to for her therapy as she put it, and she was always grateful that she had someone to be there for her like she was for so many of her other friends. I remember once a couple months before she left she even suggested that I possibly hook up with Nereida because she thought we would make a great couple. I thought her medicine was playing tricks with her mind, because I couldn't see it. She wasn't even my type and I blew her off. She had already told me she wasn't going to pick out my future bride like she did with her first bout with cancer.

Somehow I had passed her little test before I knew I was even taking it. She was confident that my decision to be with Nereida was true. This made her very happy for me, for us, and she embraced me for keeping my promise to her. I had been so far down the road in life I had forgotten the promise I made to her to love again. More importantly, I was off to a good start at living my life for me.

Want/Need

I had to have you. Your addictive ways kept my heart on a wiry shoestring. I accepted you and the bounty with which you gave, happy to finally have my jagged edges smoothed out this way. The back and forth, the to and fro was rhythmic and cyclical at a speed that made it seem we were standing still.

The nourishment of your conversation crept deep into my soul, arousing the fertility of my lost soil. It was only natural that your paths would cross one day through the road of my heart, the origin of all master plans. Take me when I say so, let me be does not mean no. I can see now how you coexist in a space meant for one. It's the left brain/ right brain acting as one. Distance and time seem not to matter. My thoughts of you are plentiful, some joyous, some painful. The random urge suppressor of any and all appetites of delight being dispensed regularly as need be without spite. I saw through the eyes of my wants what I truly needed so I'm grateful that I can live life need not wanting.

161

21

The Replenished Well

A drop, a sip, a ladle full, slow is the process to regain the level to maintain a nourished pool.

THE REPLENISHED WELL Too Tired to Stop

I've been working six days a week plus since the late spring/early summer of 1994. First with the hope of securing my first home for my family, which I did in July 1994, and then to save up for a trip to Cuba in the spring of 1995 to watch my son Lamont play baseball on a traveling team with his little brother Curt being the bat boy. In addition, I had the O.J. Simpson trial sprinkled in to keep me busy at work. I work in the broadcasting business, currently in the news department and war and scandal make for the busiest of times. Cynthia's recurrence of cancer happened right before my trip to Cuba and only a year after our reconciliation. We had been separated for 15 months and seemed to be going nowhere fast. We happened upon a counselor, after three or four previous tries with other therapist, who actually made headway in putting Cynthia and me on a path to recovery that still enables me to be strong enough to keep getting up off the mat. Her name was Dr. Dixon. We called her Priscilla. She taught me how to pace myself and I've needed it because my life has been a constant onslaught of responsibility.

Depleted from the rigors of trying to be whatever my family needed me to be, I found my soul to be tired but my mind made me forge ahead. I prayed that the hectic pace of my life would leave me further along whenever I checked to see how I was doing. I am a worker bee and never had the luxury to reflect for any sustained period of time. I grabbed what life gave me and shunned what my gut told me was wrong. Cynthia's death left me with a high of pride for her courage, and I let that propel me as far as it could. I let the inspiration of my kids fuel me as my energy waned.

It wasn't until I fell in love with Nereida that I discovered the degree to which my life had become so barren. I was living off the fumes of my emotions. Frenetic is the best way to describe my state. I felt nothing. The numbness had traveled from my heart throughout my body, and it wasn't until she touched my back that I heard the echo from the hollowness inside me. I had depth beyond my years, but it was more like a vacuum, gastric in make-up.

The instinct to punch and move is all that I know, but when I accepted Nereida to love, it gave me the fuel to run my race more realistically. I had purpose for myself on a personal level. My tiredness was more of a determined sprinter as I ran toward a better life for me with the finish line constantly being inched back a foot or two. She wanted me to stop, slow down and appreciate our life and I do. As a result, the more I reflect on the good fortune of finding such a special relationship, my thoughts elicited feelings similar to that of a person with a lucky rabbit's foot. So I rubbed it to increase the mood about my smile.

The practicality of my constraints, due to my obligation to my children, keeps my mind centered or at least with one foot on the ground as my dreams of a life with Nereida easily make me want to run away and just be happy for me. The anxiousness of becoming an individual again pushed me forward because I had spent more than half my life being responsible for others. As I learned to let my kids go little by little, as they've gotten older and matured, I've gained a stronger sense of me. I know adulthood does not end my responsibility to Lamont, Curtis, Ashley and Lyndsay, but the experience as they step further and further into the outside world comforts me and excites me as I see their growth. They have become self-sufficient young people, strong in mind, spirit and personalities. They have learned to love themselves strongly without apologizing to anyone. They understand the common thread of family, honor and responsibility to each other that is demanded. They don't have to always like each other, but they must always defend each other. Fear thy father and laugh heartily with him because we need laughter in our life to maintain.

I wait on them hand and foot not because I have to but because I want their youth to be filled with more experiences of highs than lows. I want their need to be stroked by another to be minuscule as I teach them how to negotiate the difference between the wants and needs of their life. The successes and failures so far seem unbalanced if you were to keep score. They haven't become the type of children who pick up after themselves or take the garbage out without being told. They don't wash the dishes unless they're nudged. They can and do maintain their own laundry. They do know when they should look to go hang out and how long. They know to call and establish contact when they are away from home for any length of time, and more importantly they know not to open the soda if it's in the pantry because Dad will put it in the fridge when it ready for public consumption, and never ever touch the Frosted Flakes without talking to Dad.

The tiredness that is occasionally felt usually rears its head if one of the kids falls short of their or my expectations. The question of where did I go wrong? Why would you throw it all away? Or please don't tell me you just wasted my money has to be addressed. Knowing that time will be the true testimony, I pray and carry on. I recognize their loss and adjustment emotionally has impacted their outlook on life as it has mine. So I let go of the reins so they can learn from their experience. The communication and feedback that exists between us are more than most parents receive so I embrace that aspect of the relationship to improve my decisions for them as individuals.

The completeness of my life has been attained. The balance that was necessary to allow me to be productive and happy can be summed up in one simple word: love. It has been my love for my family that has pushed me when I wanted to quit day in and day out. The love from my mother who always seemed to know when to call and say "momma loves you", the courage to pursue and secure a relationship with Nereida, love her and allow her to love me, and last but not least my love for Cynthia who in spite of the struggles of living most of her short life with me gave me a special type of love that I could use as a road map to excel, accept and better appreciate the meaning of love.

The Replenished Well

As I look inside this hole, deep, dark and alluring, each stone telling its own story connected by mortars' time. Echoes of a life well lived, it reveals a history that was once so full, measured by pebbles cast about, which can rattle to a silence or be sipped from the ladle of her touch. As seasons come and go, its popularity sometimes wanes. The rope to the bucket has been extended to measure its true barrenness. Splashes of life are faint, in dire need of natures reprieve. She pours from her infinite challis what seems to have been left behind, a tidal wave of love in her basin of amour. Ah, she sees her reflection upon the crown of my brim. The replenished well can be used again.

22

Sweet Sixteen

Coming of age, driving permits and half way to where?

Sweet Sixteen

It's been almost a year since there has been any meaningful interaction between Nereida and Ashley. Their relationship was strained at best. Ashley had become increasingly distant with Nereida as my relationship with Nereida blossomed. It wasn't just Ashley; though Lamont and Curtis were so self-involved they continued to cling to each other as they put space between their world and the life of an expanded family concept of Nereida and Lyndsay being part of our immediate family. The boys had each other; Ash had me; and Nereida was a wedge pushing her out.

Lamont had already dropped out of college and was living seven hours away in Olean, N.Y. with his girlfriend April and his baby daughter, Taylor. Lamont was retracing the steps of my youth, making decisions which affected the rest of life with a hardship he couldn't appreciate. He had always been the type of child who showed the most outward loyalty to me when he was young and the most disdain for me when his mom died. I understood the lashing out. After several years of caring for Cynthia, I knew I was the only person who would tolerate his behavior and still love him, and he needed to vent his pain and emptiness of missing his mom even if it meant his dad was the victim. He was twenty and a father; I was nineteen when he was born. He was going to show me he could do it because I did it. He had something to fill the void left behind by his mother, and he would rise above the hardships of his responsibilities because he was a Richardson and that's what we do.

Curtis flew under the radar as he always did, never putting himself in harm's way enough to register a high alert from me, even though I knew he would stray further than his brother. Curtis is a typical middle child. He loved his brother, his best friend and confidant. Where Lamont's personality was abrasive, Curtis was calm very mellow and charming. Where Lamont lashed out if struck down, Curtis was more outwardly sensitive so he cried first then lashed back with more cutting means. Curtis always gets what he wants because he is more patient in appearance. He was wedged between two A Type personalities in Lamont and Ashley so he learned early on to lie in the cut so he could get more of what he wanted. He was always the deciding vote in every family poll and showed loyalty only to his wants or needs. He didn't side with the guys, Lamont and me, unless it served him well. He was his own person at very early age and could be happy alone or in a crowd. Like his brother, though, he was a momma's boy and took his pain inward, consulting mostly with his brother and occasionally his sister. He used his vast new popularity at his new school to forge his own path of drifting from one strange embrace to another mistaking adulation for love.

Ashley, on the other hand, mourned her mom's death differently than her brothers. She exuded a feeling of betrayal. She immediately assumed the role of matriarch of the family at the age of nine. She resented her mom, though, for all the broken promises that she would have to live without. The boys had each other and she had me. She was my Molasses Princess and I treated her as such. This did cause friction and envy with her brothers, not because of what I did for her, because they were just as spoiled as her, but the pampering Ashley received from me was nonexistent for her brothers who were "Mommy's Boys" as Cynthia had labeled them and that was a void I could not fill.

The arrival of my granddaughter pulled my kids closer together, and they even began to pull Lyndsay a little into the loop. However, Nereida was becoming increasingly the enemy as I discussed my interest in having her and Lyndsay move in with us and the eventual possibility of me remarrying. The kids believed that I had changed since becoming involved and falling in love with Nereida and they didn't like it. They hated change, and if there was going to be any change in their home it would be the new parties who would have to adapt, not them. They were full of attitude and could care less if I found happiness. Ashley let me know she understood she would have to let me go one day, but she wasn't ready yet so it wasn't going to happen. I couldn't believe these were my children, but I recognized the attitude because they got it honestly from Cynthia and me. They were exerting their will on me, and they united in defiance of anything I said. Ashley was the youngest of the group and had galvanized her siblings to disrupt my master plan.

I purposely kept Nereida at bay as I "upped" our relationship. I had no intention of replacing their mom. I even thought they were grateful to me for that. Their need, though, for a maternal figure in their lives became more and more apparent as they complained. They couldn't accept that Nereida was a different style of mom than their mom. She treated them more like little adults than children. She made herself available to them only when they asked. They saw her as Dad's woman, no-more no-less. I had developed a strong relationship with Lyndsay in a very paternal way and she welcomed it, but my kids were demanding the same of Nereida as they claimed they didn't want or need her in their life.

I preached acceptance and the children gave what they perceived they were getting back. I found myself in a struggle between my life and future and neither seemed ready to concede the other's position. Although the kids were older, they were still immature in their thought processes, so I appealed to Nereida to get more involved in my kids lives. They, we, I needed to have them do more than respect her and who she was to me. We needed to work more on being a family, and she needed to build a relationship with my kids like I had with her daughter. She had her work cut out for her because I had three and she had one, but I knew the key was Ashley because the boys would move on but

Ashley was here to stay. She had become the symbol of the woman in the Richardson men's lives, and Nereida and she had to peacefully coexist if we were ever gonna really be happy later in life.

In the summer of 2001, Nereida wanted to do something big to celebrate my 40th birthday. She couldn't get the support of the kids because they knew I didn't go in for surprise parties or parties bigger than my immediate family. My spirits were low because Lamont was away struggling to raise his young family, and his health didn't seem great when we went to visit him earlier during spring break. He was working in a huge meat and produce warehouse one of only two people of color. Street in attitude and appearance, just begging for some red neck to punch his clock. He was intelligent but wore his attitude on his chest like a crest. The visit was positive because Nereida and I came to visit with Curtis, Ashley and Lyndsay. We filled their fridge the best we could and picked up all of the little things a struggling family would need. We showed pride in his quest to make it on his own and we made sure he knew. We played with the baby as we tried to get used to the feeling of being grandparents as the invitation was extended from Lamont to Nereida. She was moved and had bonded with the kids more; they let her in, and she graciously accepted it.

Lamont had mailed some new pictures of Taylor to Nereida for me for my birthday. She was supposed to frame them and get a cake for me and present them to me. Nereida picked out the two best pictures and

174

found some frames to put them in. Everyone seemed happy and this made me feel good. Nereida sized up the pictures and how she needed to trim them to fit them in the frames she purchased. Ashley suggested that Nereida not cut the pictures until after she gave them to me because she knew I would want to take them around to friends and family to show them off. Nereida thought it would take away from the presentation of them in the frame. Ashley tried to convince her and Nereida pulled rank. Lamont had sent the pictures to her, and this was what he wanted so she was going to keep her promise to Lamont. This is when Lyndsay suggested to Ashley to just take the pictures later and hide them until she could show me them. Ashley did. Nereida became frantic. First, because she thought she had lost these adorable pictures of my granddaughter, and then she realized the kids namely Ashley had something to do with them missing and her hands were tied because she couldn't accuse her of stealing the pictures so she had to let the day unfold and live with the disappointment of letting Lamont and me down.

The snowball began to roll down the hill and it became bigger and bigger as the weeks went by. Ashley escaped to Lamont's for a couple of weeks to avoid the scrutiny of the situation. Nereida was angry, hurt and humiliated by the experience, and I knew I had trouble beyond anything I had ever experienced. Ashley was avoiding an apology and Nereida had removed herself from the family. She wanted the kids to interact with her in a way which I knew they wouldn't. Ashley knew what she did was wrong but knew she did it for the right reason. It became a battle about who knew me best and what I liked or wanted. Ashley was right and Nereida was wrong about my wants. Ashley was wrong to overstep her position with an adult, but I admired her courage and conviction. I don't even remember if she ever apologized to Nereida. I had two wounded females, each demanding that I see the pain the other caused them, how they were harmed trying to love me. This was worse than being caught between my mother and wife. Ashley was a stubborn fifteen year older and could hold onto something like a hot nickel. I ignored both of them after a while because they both let a bad experience escalade into a rendition of the "Hatfield vs. Mc Coy", forgetting the bigger picture, and I was not going to allow myself to be emotionally blackmailed by either of them.

The strain on our relationship began to wear on me after six months so I began speaking and demanding a resolution to this mess. I was not going to have my life upended over a power play between my woman and my daughter. I talked with Ashley, prodded her and finally explained to her how her behavior was hurting me. I explained that Nereida was here for the duration of my life. She was the woman I had chosen to share my life with. I asked her not to be threatened by her presence because sharing me did not diminish her place in my heart. I had to get Ash to look at the bigger picture. I reminded her she would not be a teen forever and the tables will be reversed. She will be asking me to one day accept some young man who she wanted to be with who I might have reservation about. Hopefully, I would make the necessary concessions if he made her happy as Nereida did for me. Finally, I just explained that her sixteenth birthday was only weeks away, I knew she was anxious to get her drivers permit, she was gonna want to date soon because Curtis was going off to college in the fall and wouldn't be around to cramp her style, and she was going to want me to be comfortable trusting her and her judgment. I told her to be mature, think about her dad for once, and give herself a chance to have a relationship with Nereida because when she runs off into the world to live her life, this same person she's giving a hard time to now might not choose to forgive her youthful digression as easily as I would because she doesn't have to.

I did something I promised myself I would never do again. I asked Nereida to do it for me because she loved me and I needed her cooperation. I had already asked it of Ashley; now I was asking it of Nereida. I was strong emotionally now and could and would accept if they didn't respond to my pleas. Nereida agreed to reach out to Ashley again, and I hoped that Ash would not shun her.

I took off work to take Ashley for her written driver's exam. We were bounced around from window to window and scolded by a few workers like any day at the DMV. We found that one nice worker who pushed you through even though something might be out of place. Ash passed her written exam and was excited so we had to call her godmother Jennifer and give her the good news. These were the moments I cherished most as a parent, watching my children make that rite of passage throughout their lives.

Nereida wanted Ashley to meet her outside the house. She didn't want to share what she was getting Ashley with anyone; she just said call me when you get the good news. I was hesitant about them going off somewhere together, not because I didn't trust Nereida but because they were like oil and water for so long now I didn't want to see this special day have any bad memories. As I turned the corner onto my street, Nereida and Ashley were pulling off from the house. I went inside my house and prayed hard and waited.

Two hours had transpired and it was dark out. It was a little after nine o'clock and I heard their voices as they entered the house. There was laughter and giggling and thanks abound. Nereida had taken Ashley on for her first driving lesson and she was ecstatic. The olive branch had been extended and she accepted. Nereida had stepped up big time and Ashley met her halfway. I had not seen them laugh or smile together in about a year. It was the best present she got that day. At least I thought so because every girl should remember her sixteenth birthday and I know she will.

23

The Independent Woman

I know it sounds like a line but I'm not like most other guys. You just wait and see, I guess it's gonna be you, down on bended knee. Before I leave and get out your face, tell me why is it my job to pay for sins of another?

The Independent Woman

I had been taken aback by the level of compassion Nereida had shown me. It never occurred to me that she could be in need of the same. Her need for a kind ear had escaped me since she seemed so together. I had watched the growth of her as a person as she went from teary-eyed divorcee, questioning who she was as a woman, to a more self-assured, spiritually connected female. Her confidence as a woman had been shaken when her marriage broke up. She had a small child to care for and didn't know which way she was to turn. She learned to be more resilient mentally and cautious with her heart. The result, she became a more self-defined woman who knew how to embrace herself.

One of the main reasons why I was drawn to Nereida was she was a person who seemed to know who she was and I identified with that. Likewise, she was not looking for someone to help define her existence she wanted someone to complement her life. We had spent so much time talking about my wants and needs, the scars and setbacks of starting over, that it didn't appear that there was much residual effect from the pain of her divorce. She had made the necessary adjustment she needed to carry on with her life, but she was still haunted by the ending of her marriage.

Her demand for a monogamous relationship was paramount. She explained to me if we were to be together there would be no room for anyone else. She would not share me, and if I felt I needed to be elsewhere, then I should be there and spare her the pain because she would not compete with someone else for my love. This was the reason she made me date other women when I first approached her because she knew from her own experience the need for clarity I would be looking for. She knew when my confidence grew back I might not be ready for the commitment of a one-on-one relationship, and most importantly, she'd been alone for almost ten years and had a routine that left very little room for anything or anyone new.

I was supportive of her dancing with the church group, and I understood the demand of her job and the hectic nature of her life. Like everything else in life, as my feeling for her grew so did my desire to be with her every chance I could. She was impressed with the passion of my love and engulfed it every chance she could. I became first in her heart, behind her child, but this did not alter or expand the time she spent with me. I believed because we were more comfortable in our relationship, this would move me further up the food chain of her interest. I was wrong. I misplaced my role in her life by mixing fruits. Her life had purpose before I arrived and the things she involved herself with gave meaning to her personally. Dancing was her form of therapy, and the fact that it was liturgical gave it even more purpose because she maintained a strong presence with her church and God.

I had begun to make changes in my life for her and I wanted the same from her. I had to constantly beat down the resentment that would build as she got home later and later from rehearsal; especially on Friday nights because this was our only true night to be together. I wasn't proposing marriage to her but I was committed to her. I felt an unbalance in our relationship. I was chasing Nereida like I did with Cynthia. She was in constant pursuit of fulfilling her personal emotional goals. I could rationalize Nereida's actions but feelings have no logic, and she had me and I wanted her in my life more. It wasn't that I had to sit around and wait for her because I had more than enough things to do or friends to hang out with. I did wait though, because I didn't want my attitude to get the best of me and begin to boycott her because my pride was hurt.

I tried to find ways to communicate my frustration with her but we'd fight. I felt handcuffed by my inability to be heard. I had fought this battle with Cynthia in her quest for spiritual fulfillment, which was usually at the expense of time spent at home or her caring for our family and I was not about to repeat that life again. I was projecting, but there was strength in my argument. Nereida felt heaped upon and let me in on what her motivation was. It had nothing to do with me; it was God and the church that carried her in her darkest hour. She told me how she made the mistake of allowing her love for her ex-husband to shrink her identity in order to be what she thought was a "good wife", how lost she was when he left her and embarrassed that she exposed herself so meekly for love. She was not going to make the same mistake again, not for me, not for any man. She was her own woman and she loved who she had become. She flipped things back around on me, questioned my insecurity, and challenged me to examine if she was what I truly wanted because I was now indicting her for the same things that attracted me to her. She hadn't changed, just my NEEDS. She was right and I knew it but that didn't mean she didn't have to address my feelings because they were real.

I'd fallen in love with this Helen Ready "I Am Woman, Hear Me Roar," scorned once never gonna happen again woman, who wouldn't let me do anything unless she could reciprocate. I had to back up and come at her a different way. She had her demons from her past and was not about to have any repeats from me or anyone else. What I needed her to do was to see me for me, look at my track record since we were together, and take a leap of faith for our relationship. Time would be the true measure for her to gauge the strength of our relationship but she needed to take steps forward with time and not allow us to become stagnant. We had more space than most couples would need, being that we only saw each other a couple times a week. This allowed us to grow slowly without over saturating each other and monopolizing each other's time. We had to learn to trust each other and appreciate each other when we were together. That meant we had to pick and choose if we wanted to spend the few hours we had together discussing things that seemed petty in nature, comfort each other after long hard weeks of handling our responsibilities, or just plain celebrate another week under our belts. The maturity of our relationship helped us both define our roles and future aspirations together.

The honeymoon was over but the passion was alive and well. We took off the kid gloves and stopped walking on egg shells, gingerly feeling each other out. I had forgotten what it sounded like to be critiqued by my lover, the discomfort of hearing that everything about me didn't move her and that she didn't want to spend every waking moment with me. The euphoria of new love had worn off and we were living in reality. Flashbacks happened and my moods began to swing. Cynthia had become a little voice in my ear, nudging me when I lapsed back into complacent modes. I had to remember to continue to work at this relationship, or I would be doomed to repeat my life and I didn't want that. The desperation that crept up in me from time to time revealed insecurities of loss and/or failure in love. My ego would not allow me to fall on the sword again for love. Nereida was definitely the woman I wanted to spend my life with, but I couldn't let love make me weak again. I took a stance with Nereida about what I wanted and needed from her. I wanted her to examine whether she saw me playing a greater role in her life. I wanted her to make our relationship more of a priority in her life, without scheduling me into her life as she currently did. I wanted her to be more involved in my personal life, with my friends and the kids. I wanted her to show an interest in things that I enjoyed like I did for her. I reminded her why we were together and how we gave the other freedom to be who we wanted to be without pretense. I reminded her that this was what kept the relationship fresh and each of us invigorated.

The Independent Woman

The independent woman sits on her throne; the independent woman chooses to stand on her own. The independent woman speaks her own mind; the independent woman when willing will oblige. She is the leader of industry, family and friend. Cloaked in a shawl of spirituality I bow to commend. Eyes, which sparkle, aura of passion, she loves better than she gets not to be outdone by a mere man. She is his equal, the match he was destined to meet, so she holds her position never giving an inch. Armed and well trained in the art of love, winning most battles only losing one. That is they retreated before the job was done. As she stands before the threshold of her biggest defeat, fist clenched tight, teeth beginning to grind, she looks into the eyes of her opponent of love her dream come true. She flails her heart, unsure if this is right. Her opponent captures her as she closes her eyes shut, only to slowly open them and finds this is some DEEP SHIT. He is an able foe sent out on his own mission. He is that of a true man never to be outdone.

The Self-Sufficient Man

I am looking for that independent woman who seems to be who you say you are. All I offer is freedom from the burden of the low ceiling of life. I have no problem if you lead, trail or stand by my side. I do ask though that you respect my mind. My record speaks for itself; lover, protector and provider. I can even make you laugh if your heart desires. So instead of standing alone as an independent woman, allow me to emancipate you, give you the freedom your heart truly desires, being my independent bride is all that is required.

24

The Torch Carrier

I found the place you told me to go to. Your directions were great, but I confess it was the trail of light cast upon my heart's wall that led the way. At times I close my eyes to take in your fragrant prompts as cues to know what to do. I am the keeper of your light, life line secured.

Epiphany of Love

My eyes were closed shut from the mortar of my tears; the congestion in my heart left a beat in dire need of respiratory care. The air surrounding me smelled unfamiliar of distance and longing my axe to bear. The numbness of taste and touch after our final embrace left my soul scalded a burn victim of a life love affair. Emotional solitaire became my game of choice, with the mirrors to my heart covered in lace shawls of fear. My retreat became deeper, my determination weaker, my soul curled in the fetal position, a new low point of despair. Along came a new friend from a long time ago she introduced herself as Epiphany, the 2nd goddess of love. She brewed me a concoction of kindness, sensibility and laughter to sip. She helped me do push ups when my moods were remiss. As my ailing heart began to mend, it was news to me that there was space for another. I misjudged the juggle my heart would have to do; the demand of my conscience, the seduction of the sub mind, each worthy of my attention at any given time. They showed no adversarial competitiveness, each seeming to know when to go or stay. I find myself thrust into an old fashioned love triangle with a different spin, a soul awakened, and a heart filled with hope. Compliments of Epiphany, the mistress of love.

A Love Triangle

This is not your typical triangle. There exists three parties, one male, two female, but it's a ménage a trois with a different spin. Both women know each other quite well and I love them both dearly. They agreed to the situation more out of necessity than desire. Their love for me allowed me to experience love in a three-dimensional setting. The question of whether a man could love two women at once was a moot point. Their similarities aren't obvious but their needs were alike, which is why I was drawn inherently to both of them. They were free spirits, people who had to fly because there was a calling inside their souls. I had these same desires but never allowed myself to soar beyond my inner dreams. There exists some envy of the other, but it's only natural as they define their space inside my heart. The surreal feelings that evolved from my experience are that the heart and mind know what it wants, what it need and this can be like blinders if the conscience is not active in its conversation with the subconscious.

Starting over was a process that did not follow any timeline or script. The only prerequisite was that I put myself out there to engage in taking resumes. My wants and needs were not clouded by moods of grief or desperation. They were instead more clear and defined because of the struggles I had gone through with Cynthia. Our relationship had many highs and lows, and fortunately for me, we were on an upswing as we had patched up our marriage before we learned of the relapse of her

189

disease. The struggles to communicate still existed, but we were better than we had been in years. The area of trust was better than shaky, but we had matured to the point where we dealt more in the here and now. We no longer had to sling accusations and innuendos back and forth at one another. We learned to show more respect for the other person and reconnected emotionally with each other. The fact that we were not in a blissful state of our marriage when we learned of the return of the cancer forced us to concentrate on doing things right. I was grateful that we had decided to reconcile before the bad news, or I'm sure Cynthia would not have agreed to make our marriage work. She hated pity and didn't want it. The separation, which lasted fifteen months, had exposed her vulnerability to making it on her own. My presence and involvement in the kids lives were a huge void at the end of the evening because we were routine in the way we lived our life. When I wasn't coming off as a pining, angry husband, she could remember why she loved me so much.

The resurgence of building my marriage over, addressing my wants, needs and the close proximity of Cynthia's death better prepared for what it would take for me to have the type of relationship I desired, not just with Cynthia, but any woman. My concerns were whether I had anything left in me to give. Did I want to put myself through the trials and tribulations of having a meaningful relationship again? Maybe the real issue was I knew love could be draining, and I definitely felt tapped out. The scars were vivid and I liked it that way. I didn't want to repeat my mistakes if I was lucky enough to find love again, but I knew to respect it better than I had in my past.

The bridge between my lost love and found love was my honesty with myself. The ability to think more with my big head and not my little head made making my decisions clear. This was no easy feat to pull off because testosterone has a way of causing a hallucinogenic state, which can leave a man in a world in which he is unprepared to live. I had been through too much already in my short life to let my penis make this decision so I put in writing what I wanted and needed and studied and repeated this mantra to myself in order to maintain the focus necessary to attain happiness one day. That day was sooner than I thought because after an innocent conversation with a good friend, I found what I was looking for. She was energetic about her life passions and I knew this translated into her being. I looked at this woman for the first time that evening, and I felt things that went beyond any physical longing. It was an epiphany that I was experiencing and I knew it.

I look back now at all the little things, the signs, the poems, and love letters I wrote to Nereida and realized these could have easily been written to Cynthia during better times of our life, but they weren't to Cynthia. They were Nereida's words because she had released thoughts and desires that I had forgotten existed in me. Death has matured me. It has made me more insightful and more deliberate in my actions. I was never whimsical or spontaneous in my approach to life before Cynthia passed away, and she constantly hammered me for it. My creativity in our relationship saved me most times, though, because I was good at planning things out, it was the engineer in me. I never needed to hang my life off a cliff to gain exhilaration from anything we did so I learned not to broadcast my every move to give a better illusion that my actions were spontaneous when they were lacking.

The lessons I learned from the loss of Cynthia are humbling. I've never tried to deny the enormity of my love for her no matter how difficult our relationship was, but even in her absence my love for her still grows. It is a history of love after the fact, not romanticized to paint a pretty picture for my mind to see. Instead, it's a more detailed acceptance of how much she became a part of my fabric. I have many reasons to close the door on that chapter of my life and never look back, but I know this would be the biggest lie I could tell my heart. She has become a partner in my conscious decisions, occupying a perch on my shoulder as my guardian angel as opposed to the devil of an imp she was in my life. She never believed that I gave her thoughts or opinions much weight or consideration in our relationship and that was completely wrong. The sacrifices made in my life were always to give her what she said she wanted or needed. It was when I knew that I couldn't gain a better situation for us that I held my ground, which meant I'd lose her support. I spoiled this woman rotten and enjoyed every minute of it. The repercussion of those actions is what undermined our relationship. I loved being the knight in shining armor because it made her beam and my ego expand even more, if that was possible. The maturity that was needed to keep things in perspective was lacking in our relationship, and this constantly skewed our vision and aspiration for sustained happiness.

In came Nereida, subtle in demeanor, more passionate than the eyes could imagine. She had the advantage/disadvantage of years of stories of my shortcomings as told by Cynthia. Nereida had no interest in playing second fiddle to another woman, especially a ghost. My need to reveal myself to her fully in my most vulnerable state gave me a chance to convince her of my emotional stability, as I tried to win her heart. She elicited raw passion, which I was convinced died more than a lifetime ago. I was developing the continuation of something I found I truly wanted, a grown-up relationship. The respect was already in place and our compatibility was already known, so I conceded to give love another try with Nereida because I believed I was better equipped to handle it at this stage in my life. I am confident I have found the right woman to share it with and continue to nourish our relationship.

We grew with each other as we slowly developed a trust in the other's words and actions. We do not dismiss what we previously knew about the other. We decided to write our own tale of love. We are aggressive in our hearts for each other, but time is our best ally because it allows us to shift and conform as we progress in our newfound relationship. We are not high school teenagers smitten by first love, although we come off that way. We are two independent people who have found in each other a complement of love, companionship, admiration and respect, which causes a euphoric sense of newness not lost on our scared hearts. We appeal to the need of each other's desires while we fill the void of wants that have mounted over a lifetime. We are blessed because we had the courage to step forward and make a relationship surrounded by scandal of our past relationship with each other's significant other a null and void issue. We are not some modern versions of "Bob and Carol, Ted and Alice" as others seemed to want to believe. We are two people who respect each other's past well enough to leave it at the back door. It gives us insight at times to the emotional chips on our shoulders and we are the better for it.

I no longer feel the need to share every emotional upheaval regarding Cynthia with Nereida, and this makes for a better relationship. Nereida is a good friend to me, but she is my woman first and I have to constantly remind myself of that because my first instinct is to share my every thought with her. Although she will hear me out, it is no longer sensible to report every detail of my thought, as I did during the infant stages of our relationship. There does not exist a pining away for lost love as one might think, just a strong sense of appreciation that my heart is able to withstand its demand. The honesty that comes from this experience gives me clarity of the impact love has made in my life and the need to enjoy it and embrace it. Cynthia made me promise her I would give love another shot, and I have, and this was truly one of the most selfless acts a person could give to another in her situation. So when I find myself bitter, angry or dismayed by Cynthia's absence in my life, after all I sacrificed for her and our happiness, I take comfort in her gift to me to love again. I am free from any and all guilt, unlike so many in my shoes. This epitomizes what has become the best measuring stick of the depth to which we loved each other and why my love for Cynthia grows as my life with Nereida blossoms. I know I would not have the emotional freedom to love on the level I do now with Nereida had Cynthia not placed me there.

The Torch Carrier

As I jog down the pathway of life all alone, the initial cheering, encouragement and kind words seem familiar and alluring. Quickly they fade along this fan lined street, no longer do they show me the way, and the markers along my route become distorted and wane. There is no runner's high, only those who've been there. The background of the crowd is occasionally heard. I carry on and act out all those requests we last spoke of, with the hope your words will bring solace to my soul. People often walk by me shaking their heads in confusion or disbelief, often giving stares as I lumber about. I break stride from my everyday life whenever you whisper in my mind. The lucidity of our conversation never denied. I have not strayed from my driven path, led instead by the brilliance of my internal light. It's what I use to pay homage to lengthen your life. Forgotten by most remembered by one, I smile in amazement of your infinite growth as I thank our love for nominating me to such an exclusive club. It is not a job that you select. It chooses you with a weight calibrated by perspective and hues. I am honored to bear the title bestowed on few; The Torch Carrier Caretaker to you.

THANKS

I would like to thank my father and mother, Thomas Harvey Richardson and Claretha Richardson Mc Kay, for instilling in me the value of self-worth and love. Mom I'd also like to say thanks for the countless occasions you walked and talked me through my journey, you being a Torch Carrier yourself since 1977. I am the man I am today because you knew how to combine the right amount of love, praise and strength while releasing the apron string long enough for me to fly, and then soar as a person. Dr.Ravikumar, Dr. Nora Farkouh, Dr. Fort, Dr. Provenzano and Mary Jo for your care of Cynthia and the insight regarding the kids over the years. I want to thank the numerous family and friends whose support and involvement in and out of my life has aided me in raising my children when it appeared I was doing it all alone. I thank God for blessing me with these people, groups and organizations, which became surrogate eyes, ears and voices of reason to my most cherished ones Lamont, Cutis, Ashley, Lyndsay and Taylor. The list goes in no order or sequence: The Mt. Vernon Razorbacks Football and Cheerleading Squads, The Mt. Vernon Little League Coaches, Traphagen Elementary School of Mt. Vernon, Brenda Smith and the staff at Mt. Vernon High School, Rye Country Day School Faculty, Coaching Staff and Parents who made Ashley and Curtis a part of your families, my colleagues at NBC, Inc. MJ(Xena) and especially the Midnight Marauders, Nel and Jacob for the cover sketches, Connie and all the staff at AWH, Dr. Gluck, Marilyn, Steph, Keisha and all my ladies at WSW thanks for keeping the Boss lady sane for me, Rosi P my second favorite PR who was my biggest supporter and fan before everyone came around, Tony, Bea and Gina of Great American Video of Mt. Vernon, The Carters, Mays, Jenkins, Phipps (all Al's free golf lesson), Santana's (Juan for all the pictures and support), Alston's and Mitchell's thanks for all the free food the kids hit you up for. Kenny and Lisa for all the free invites to the barbeques and Phil for watching even though your hands were full and La Wanda for the one on ones at City Island. To Jenny Mc the Best Godmother a parent could ask for. You've kept Ash in check the way she needed to be and me with perspective only a true friend could give. Thanks Mary and Michael, for allowing Curtis and Ashley to be part of the Jackson family and Nikki, Vanessa and PJ for putting up with them. G of NC via Queens, Shirl C. for not forgetting me, Tammy for all the long distance check ups, Gladys and Anthony your timely cards and calls always make it seem like you're still near and Hudson, Mass. is right around the corner. My big sisters Ross and Gwen, you've been just that and I love you for knowing me the way you guys do, and Charlie Rob, we're more brother than we know but we always got room for Joe. Moody, my favorite uncle, thanks for keeping things light. The Duberstein family for all the laugh and Donald for getting me kick started and referring me to Jo Fagan, Ji Young for inspiring me as you grab hold of your dreams, Stephen King for giving me the courage to just do, Steph G for all the inspirational talks and laughs, Tim "Saxs" my barber for the kind ear and connections like PR guru Terri Williams who sent me to Adrienne Ingram who sent me to Malaika Adero who convince me to go with my thoughts and Dave "Big Daddy" Farris and all the other quality individuals from the shop. To the Staff at Home Run City thanks for all the reps in the cages for the kids. Lil' sis Lea, keep looking ahead because I got your back. The Stiths' for giving life to Cynthia and making her the unique person she turned out to be. Aunt Louise and Aunt Thelma, your words have always carried a lot of weight and I hear you. Aunt Doris, Jo and Bae thanks for being there, especially for my mom. Mary W. and Cathy D for feeling my pain, the Moores for not letting the kids drift too far away from the family (Can and Yell don't get lost), my nephew Shyron, Cory and Rodney step and take care of your mom. Tray for coming back to NY with Jordan and Taylor and Ms. Gill for letting me through your front door, Donna and Kyle for allowing me to continue to retreat to your home and include me in the Ogle/ Williams family, Maritza for helping your sister believe in second chances, April for being a part the family

199

and giving us Taylor, Lamont, Curtis, Ashley and Lyndsay you make my life worth living and I thank you guys for showing some interest in me completing this project. To my surrogates La Shawna, Marshall, Josh, Jake, James, Joi, Lelani, Brian R., Allison S., Tal, Dan R., Dubbie, Paul F., Max, Brandon I love you guys and appreciate that you treated me so well but if you all did the backyard I'd truly feel your love. Cass thanks for being CLUTCH and last but not least Nereida, for being a friend when my voice went silent and my screams were loud.

About the Author

Antonio Richardson has worked the last 20 years in the Broadcast Industry. He began his career as a Broadcast System Design Engineer but after some restructuring within his company found himself in the operational end of the business. This change coincided with a major changes in his personal life. He and his wife Cynthia had just passed the remission stage of her bout with Breast Cancer and Antonio was returning to work after an extended absence due to a company strike. Antonio found himself financially and emotionally spent. It was during this period that Antonio turned to writing to get a grip on his life as a husband, father and possible widower that he found the inner calm of reflection and an old love for writing. So he continued to write over the next 15 years sharing his words with only a select few. After the death of his wife Cynthia writing became more of a means of survival and later the voice he used to articulate his emotions when he had to start his life anew. Thus leading him to The Torch Carrier a memoir which started out as a compilations of letters poems and sonnets which when strung together told the story and transformation of his life and battle of lost and found. Antonio continues to work in the television and has held various jobs. He is currently an Operation's Supervisor at NBC, Inc. for The Today Show with Katie Couric and Matt Lauer, The Weekend Today Show and on occasion Nightly News with Tom Brokaw. As his professional life became ever changing and exposing him more to the power of text so has his passion for writing, thus leading Antonio to consider writing as more than just a recreational or therapeutic aspect of his life.

He has maintained residence in Westchester County of New York just 15 miles north of Manhattan where he resides with his family. Still surrounded by his core of friends and extended family members who watch over him. His family has expanded by two and half with Nereida and her daughter Lyndsay and occasionally Taylor his granddaughter as Lamont, Curtis and Ashley have grown into normal young adults with all the angst that follow.

Printed in the United States
35174LVS00003B/200

9 781410 796974